# eccentric finger lakes

a curious guide to

offbeat history

entirely factual

astonishing

natural spectacles

out of the ordinary

restaurants, wineries, and lodgings

hidden treasures

most unusual and

unexpected things to do

For T

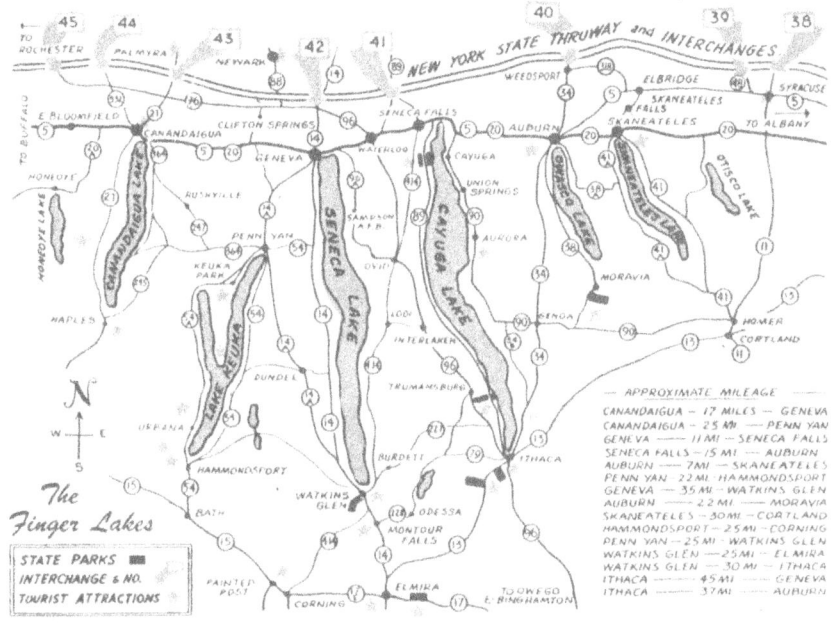

There's no place on earth quite like the Finger Lakes, and there's never been a book about the region quite like this one.

An exceptionally beautiful 4,692-square-mile corner of Upstate New York, the Finger Lakes is dotted with historic cities, vast farmland, lush vineyards, dramatic gorges and waterways. But perhaps most intriguing are the region's many eccentricities, beginning with Native American folklore. The earliest inhabitants believed the lakes were formed when the Great Spirit laid his hands on the land to bless it, and His fingers left imprints that filled with water. In fact, the lakes all bear names derived from Native American languages.

*Eccentric Finger Lakes* is an armchair travel guide of sorts to the odd, the offbeat, the fascinating, the mysterious, and the just plain unexpected. This book explores the region's often overlooked stories and treasures, bizarre legends and best-kept secrets. It's filled with curious characters – religious zealots, mediums, daredevils, explorers, suffragettes, inventors,

1

benefactors, artists and writers, winemakers and chefs, bootleggers and scoundrels. Women include the local school teacher who survived a trip over Niagara Falls in a barrel, the first female Space Shuttle Commander, the first woman to receive a medical degree in the United States, the mother of grape pies, and the woman on the twenty dollar bill. Among the men, the first American abstract painter, the man who purchased Alaska, the fellow who put the basket in basketball, the man who gave away $35,000 worth of dimes, and the professor who invented Chicken McNuggets.

This place has given birth to the time clock, motion picture talkies, the ice cream sundae, granola, French bread pizza, the electric chair, cast iron plow, craft coffee, fiber optic cable, the fire hydrant, stuffed toys, bloomers, utopian societies, world-class universities, Planned Parenthood, the Pledge of Allegiance, and Memorial Day. Finger Lakes cities made movies before Hollywood and provided inspiration for *It's a Wonderful Life's* Bedford Falls. Works including *Tom Sawyer*, *Huckleberry Finn*, *Lolita*, *Cosmos*, and episodes of *The Twilight Zone* were written here. Songs including "Puff the Magic Dragon" and "Stardust" were composed here.

Turn the pages and visit the town that has a church on every corner, an abandoned insane asylum, the most enlightened city in America, the largest landfill in New York State, the smallest state park, waterfalls taller than Niagara, a haunted winery, a brain collection, and the Dalai Lama's North American retreat. Drive through a covered bridge, under a bridge to nowhere, and over a hill that defies gravity. Search for a yellow-bellied sapsucker, a Gothic Castle, the lady in granite, a restaurant in the middle of nowhere, a two-story outhouse, and "Old Greeny," the legendary lake creature. Discover the drive-in that time forgot, the best place to pick strawberries, a bar that hands out $2 bills, a buried Viking village, a Volkswagen made of stone, and find out what in the world Amelia Earhart was doing here.

When you put all these tales and stories together, it's like a curtain has been lifted, and it's hardly surprising that this particular place has been called quirky and improbable, curious and scandalous, grand and inventive — all those things and more.

Whether you read this book straight through, or pick out individual stories as the mood strikes, you're in for a captivating read!

# THE TWELFTH LAKE

Long, narrow and somewhat parallel bodies of water, oriented north to south, the eleven Finger Lakes from west to east are Conesus, Hemlock, Canadice, Honeoye, Canandaigua, Keuka, Seneca, Cayuga, Owasco, Skaneateles and Otisco. But there is another lake, not far away, created by the same glacial ice sheets that carved out the Finger Lakes. Silver Lake, near the village of Perry and Letchworth State Park, is three miles long and a half-mile wide, surrounded by sloping hills, and sharing the same north-south orientation of the other Finger Lakes. Yet Silver Lake's orphan status is likely due to its location west of the Genesee River. Silver Lake has one unusual feature the other lakes do not — both the inlet and outlet are at the northern end of the lake.

*Factoid*: Two smaller bodies of water east of Keuka Lake, Waneta and Lamoka Lakes, drain south and empty into the Cohocton River and Susquehanna system, and eventually into the Chesapeake, which is why they are not considered Finger Lakes. Because of their modest size, Waneta and Lamoka are called the "Finger Nail" Lakes.

# EARTH'S CAPITAL?

Extraterrestrial intelligence interested in our planet would be most likely to visit Ithaca. The "Voyager One" spacecraft, passing far beyond the solar system, carries a 12-inch golden phonograph record that contains 115 images, music from different cultures and eras, and spoken greetings from Earth-people in fifty-five languages, intended as an interstellar message to any alien civilization that may recover the Voyager. Since these were compiled by Carl Sagan at Cornell University, an intelligent alien would infer that Earth's capital (and appropriate landing site) is Ithaca.

*Factoid*: In the most recent fifteen-year sample period, the Finger Lakes region had 394 officially reported UFO sightings.

# FAKE NEWS

Millard Fillmore was born on January 7, 1800 in a log cabin on a farm in what is now the town of Moravia in Cayuga County. In 1823 he was admitted to the bar, practiced law in Buffalo, and later served as a member of the House of Representatives. In 1848, he was elected Vice President on a ticket with Zachary Taylor, and thrust into the presidency after Taylor's death in 1850. On December 28, 1917, an article by H. L. Mencken in *The New York Evening Mail* claimed that when the bathtub was first introduced into the United States in 1842, there was widespread public opposition, but that changed after President Fillmore had one installed in the White House in 1850, giving the bathtub recognition and respectability. Mencken's article was fascinating. It was also completely false. He made the whole thing up, partly for entertainment during the bleak days of World War I, but also to make a point about how quickly a lie can become conventional wisdom.

*Factoid*: In honor of Fillmore's apocryphal adoption of the bathtub, the town of Moravia celebrated "Fillmore Days" with four-wheeled bathtub races down Main Street, beginning in 1975. The event was dropped in the 90s citing the danger of a rogue bathtub flying off course.

# HOW DO YOU LIKE THEM APPLES?

For more than a century, Cornell University's Agricultural Experiment Station in Geneva has been home to pomologists devoted to improving and propagating new varieties of tree fruit. Varieties from Cortland to Jonagold and Empire, were developed in Geneva. Thanks to the station's scientists, New York is second only to Washington State in apple production. Sales of Cornell Orchards-grown apples and other fresh fruit at the Orchards Farm Store (709 Dryden Road in Ithaca) support ongoing research.

*Factoid*: Pioneer nurseryman John Chapman, popularly known as

"Johnny Appleseed," passed through the Finger Lakes on his way from Massachusetts to Ohio. Sometimes he handed out seeds to travelers, other times dropping seeds along the way. As the years passed, apple orchards grew all along the shores of the lakes, and near hundreds of other rivers and streams.

## BOGIE'S SUMMER VACATION

Humphrey Bogart's father, Dr. Belmont Bogart was born in Watkins Glen, and his mother Maud was a native of Rochester. Although they lived in New York City, where Dr. Bogart practiced medicine, the family, including young Humphrey, spent summers from 1899 to 1916 at a 55-acre estate on Canandaigua Lake, eight miles south of Canandaigua village. During the summer of 1914, fifteen-year-old Humphrey saved Arthur Hamlin, grandson of the local banker, from drowning after he fell off the dock at Seneca Point.

*Factoid*: By coincidence, Ingrid Bergman was a frequent visitor to Canandaigua Lake during the time she lived in Rochester with her first husband, a professor at the University of Rochester. She left the area in 1941, shortly before appearing in the legendary film *Casablanca* in which she co-starred with – you guessed it – Humphrey Bogart.

## SPOOK HILL

A strange phenomenon can be experienced on a hill in the small town of Middlesex, just east of Canandaigua Lake. The location on Newell Road has come to be known as "Spook Hill." At the peak of the road, just as the pavement appears to decline, a car stopped in neutral will roll backwards uphill, defying laws of gravity. Many believe it's just an optical illusion or Earth's magnetic forces at work. Others think the cause is more supernatural in nature. Stories tell of an old Native American burial ground near

Spook Hill and that spirits of those passed are pushing cars back up. Factoid: A "gravity hill" is a spot in the road where the layout of surrounding land and landmarks creates an optical illusion, making a slight downhill slope appear to be an uphill slope. Despite solid proof, the mystery and history surrounding Spook Hill continues to draw attention from people around the world.

## WHALE OF A TALE

On June 5, 1888, Captain Thomas Gibson Nickerson harpooned a 75-ton, 65-foot-long fin whale off the coast of Cape Cod and lugged it to shore. Since a whale was something most Americans of the time had never seen, he preserved the great mammal with 1,500 gallons of embalming fluid, and embarked on a traveling exhibition in which he charged admission for viewing. Over the next year Nickerson exhibited her across seven states. After sailing up the Cayuga-Seneca Canal to Waterloo, the structure that housed the whale caught fire, and, accelerated by the volatile chemicals inside her large veins, the whale was badly burned. On further transport through the Erie Canal and into Lake Ontario, the barge capsized, and the carcass sank to the bottom of the lake.

*Factoid*: Captain Nickerson returned to sea after the ill-fated exhibition, serving on other whaling ships. He eventually retired to his summer home on Keuka Lake near Penn Yan, where he wrote stories of his whaling adventures.

## THE REAL BEDFORD FALLS

Named for the series of small falls and rapids on the Seneca River which drains both Cayuga and Seneca Lakes, Seneca Falls is presumed to be Frank Capra's inspiration for Bedford Falls in his 1946 classic film *It's a Wonderful Life*. Capra visited Seneca Falls in the 1940s, and while he never acknowledged the connection, similarities between the real town and the fictional version are many. Rochester, Buffalo, and Elmira are all mentioned in the movie and referenced as being fairly close. Besides geographical location, much of the architecture is strikingly similar, especially the steel truss bridge. Originally, Harry Bailey attends Cornell University, located in nearby Ithaca, however, the studio recommended not referring to the college by name and that detail was cut from the movie. Bailey Park in the film was built by the Bailey Building and Loan, providing affordable, decent housing for working-class families. Similarly, nineteenth century industrialist and Seneca Falls resident, John Rumsey, built and sold affordable homes for his employees in what is still called Rumseyville. And local businessman Norman J. Gould, one of the richest men in town, had great control over politics and economics of the area, much as Henry F. Potter did in the movie. You can take a walk across the bridge over Cayuga-Seneca Canal, a close match to the bridge that George Bailey jumped from to save Clarence the angel. A plaque on the bridge proclaims it as one of the many similarities to the fictional town of Bedford Falls.

*Factoid*: Bronze stars embedded in the sidewalks along 15 blocks of Hollywood Boulevard, the "Hollywood Walk of Fame," were made by the Knight Letter Works (later known as Matthews International Corporation) on Chestnut Street in Seneca Falls until 1975.

## How to Find True Love

Commissioned in 1925 by millionaire manufacturer Elmer J. Bliss, the sailing vessel Venona II was built in Wiscasset, Maine by Pendleton Brothers Shipyard. In 1940, the schooner was renamed "True Love" in the 1940 romantic comedy *The Philadelphia Story* with Cary Grant and Katherine Hepburn, where she appeared as a miniature model of herself, and in Katharine Hepburn words, "My, she was yar." Sixteen years later the True Love made her life size debut in *High Society*, the musical remake

9

of *The Philadelphia Story* with Bing Crosby, Grace Kelly and Frank Sinatra. In the film, Bing Crosby serenades Grace Kelly with the song "True Love" while onboard True Love. For three decades, the True Love sailed the Caribbean, then in 2008 she was purchased by Josh and Lisa Navone of Watkins Glen. Today, a fully restored True Love sails from the southern end of Seneca Lake.

*Factoid*: The True Love operates as a passenger boat, certified by the Coast Guard for up to 22 passengers. Schooner Excursions offers four trips daily from Seneca Harbor Park Pier.

## WE ARE STARDUST

As you drive along Route 54 south of Penn Yan, you pass the unmarked site of the old Keuka Hotel near the foot of Hyatt Hill in the town of Wayne (named in honor of Revolutionary War hero General Anthony Wayne), built on the lakeshore by James Washburn in 1894 and demolished in 1974. Rudyard Kipling and Arthur Conan Doyle were both early guests of the hotel. Hoagy Carmichael was the pianist and vocalist in the hotel ballroom during the 1926 and 1927 seasons, and local legend has it that he wrote "Stardust" during his time at the hotel.

*Factoid*: Called "a song about a song about love," Carmichael's "Stardust" became an American standard, the most recorded song of the 20th century.

## THE SUBJECT WAS ROSES

It was in the Wayne County village of Newark that Albert E. Jackson and his son-in-law, Charles H. Perkins, fruit growers and amateur gardeners, established the Jackson and Perkins Company in 1872. In 1884 they hired E. Alvin Miller, a professional propagator and breeder, and the company began to cultivate roses on a large scale. In 1908, they received an award from the National Rose Society for the popular "Dorothy Perkins" climbing rose (named for Charles' granddaughter). During the 1920s and 30s the company developed hundreds of new varieties and sold millions of plants. During World War II the largest rose grower in the world folded in Germany, leaving the door open for Jackson and Perkins to become the world's rose garden.

*Factoid*: Newark was the home of writer Charles Reginald Jackson, best known for his 1944 novel *The Lost Weekend*, the autobiographical novel chronicling a struggling writer's five-day drinking binge. The 1945 film version, directed by Billy Wilder and starring Ray Milland and Jane Wyman, won that year's Best Picture Oscar.

## PURPLE PASSION

Southwest of Canandaigua Lake, Naples has become the "Grape Pie Capital of the World." It was Al Hodges, owner of the Redwood Restaurant in Naples, who introduced the novelty of pies made with locally-abundant Concord grapes in 1965. When he couldn't keep up with the demand, Hodges enlisted the help of Irene Bouchard who operated a small local baking business in her home. By the time she retired, she was called the "Mother of Grape Pies," making more than 10,000 pies a year during the autumn months when Concords are available. The seasonal dessert is labor intensive, since each individual grape needs to be squeezed between thumb and forefinger to separate pulp and skins. Today, Monica Schenk of Monica's Pies is the best-known grape pie baker in the region, selling 10,000 pies a year, freezing 10 tons of grape pulp to use year round.

*Factoid*: Practically everything is purple in Naples – the fire hydrants, doors of the community theater, cars, flags on the main street of town, and several Victorian homes.

# VIEW FROM THE TOP

There's arguably one place that provides the best view of the influence of glaciers in sculpting the U-shaped valleys and steepened hillsides of the Finger Lakes region. That must-visit spot is called "The Jump Off," the highest point in Ontario County at 2,256 feet, located on Gannett Hill in Ontario County Park in Naples. From an elevated platform, the lookout on the Finger Lakes Trail at Gannett Hill in Naples provides panoramic views of Bristol Valley on the western horizon, and on clear days, it's possible to see all the way to Seneca and Cayuga Lakes to the east.

*Factoid*: The hill was named to honor Frank Gannett, the region's newspaper mogul and unsuccessful Republican candidate for Governor of New York in 1936.

# SWEDE DREAMS

According to urban legend, Ithaca has the largest per capita inventory of serviceable Volvos of any city outside of Sweden, the local vehicle of choice for durability, reliability and longevity. With super-warm heating systems, Volvos make great "winter rat" cars, needing only a good set of snow tires to navigate the hilly local terrain. One can usually find an old Volvo in Ithaca inexpensively and drive it almost indefinitely.

*Factoid*: Since 1974, Dave Brumsted's Ithaca Foreign Car Service, housed in an unexpectedly posh timber-frame structure at 501 West State Street, has kept most of Ithaca's Volvos on the roads.

# SMALLEST STATE PARK

Squaw Island is located at the north end of Canandaigua Lake, near the city of Canandaigua, one of only two islands in the Finger Lakes. Although frequently described as New York's smallest state park, it is not formally designated as a state park, rather it is a "unique area" managed by the New York State Department of Environmental Conservation. Flint arrowheads and other artifacts found on the island suggest that the first humans who settled in the region, ancestors of the Iroquois tribe, used the island for hunting waterfowl and deer.

*Factoid*: There are continuing efforts to change its name, as with other places with "squaw" in the name, since the use of the term is now considered insensitive.

## OLD SPARKY

In 1889, Edwin R. Davis, the Auburn Prison electrician designed an electric chair, fitted with electrodes applied to the head and leg, and powered by a second-hand generator purchased and shipped to Auburn from Brazil after George Westinghouse had refused to sell any of his generators for use in electrocutions. On August 6, 1890, convicted murderer William Kemmler became the first person sent to the chair. After he was strapped in, a charge of 700 volts was delivered for only 17 seconds before the current failed. The second charge was 1,030 volts and applied for about two minutes, and Kemmler was pronounced dead. "They would have done better using an axe," declared Westinghouse. The assassin of President William McKinley, anarchist Leon Czolgosz, was executed on October 29, 1901 in the Auburn Prison electric chair.

*Factoid*: Gustav Stickley was foreman of Auburn Prison's furniture plant when it was common for private companies to contract with the state to use convict labor to produce goods, and in 1890 he was called upon to build that first electric chair. Stickley later became one of the principal figures in the American Arts and Crafts movement and creator of Craftsman-style furniture.

# Follow the Yellow Brick Road

The yellow-hued bricks originally used to pave a stretch of State Street in Ithaca were sourced from a brickworks which used clay with less iron than clay that produced more typical orange or red bricks. As a young performer in a traveling theater troupe, Lyman Frank Baum arrived in Ithaca to court Maud Gage, a young woman from Fayetteville who attended Cornell. Legend has it that when Baum asked for directions to the university he was told to "follow the yellow brick road." He made his way up to East Hill, and in 1900 he immortalized the "yellow brick road" in his best-selling children's book, *The Wonderful Wizard of Oz*.

*Factoid*: When the old bricks were torn up and replaced with more-common red bricks, the yellow bricks were re-used to build the house at 1114 East Shore Drive in 1939 (by coincidence, the very same year MGM's film version of *The Wizard of Oz* was released).

# Brotherhood of the Blades

In 1861, a young soldier named Wyman Johnson flung the blade of a farmer's scythe into a balsam poplar tree in front of his home in Waterloo and walked off to join the Civil War. He told his mother he would retrieve it when he returned. He died in the war, and his implement stayed in the tree. In 1918, two other members of the family hung their scythes in the same tree as they went off to fight in World War I. They did not return. Today there are three scythes imbedded in the tree in somber tribute to those who went off to war and never came back.

*Factoid*: The original scythe, barely visible as the old tree has almost swallowed it up, has become a curious roadside attraction on Route 5 half-way between Waterloo and Geneva (mail box number is 841). All three blade tips have been painted so the passerby can easily find them in the trunk of the 100-foot tall tree.

# STICKY BUNS

Folks driving through the Finger Lakes might consider the Steuben County town of Bath a quick stop for a bathroom break, or for that matter, pass by altogether. Those people would miss a small, local gathering place at 28 Liberty Street that has been in operation since 1993. The employees at Chat-a-Whyle still talk about the day Hedy Lamarr, the Hollywood bombshell MGM called "the most beautiful woman in the world," stopped in for sticky buns. Made from a secret recipe, the restaurant's butter-soaked, caramel-covered buns, baked in-house daily, are legendary throughout the region.

*Factoid*: The county seat of Steuben County, Bath is either named after the city in England or after Lady Bath, daughter of William Pulteney, one of the area's original landowners.

# ATOMIC HOMEFRONT

The Finger Lakes has a little-known nuclear past as a storage center for radioactive materials in connection with the Manhattan Project, and despite no formal confirmation from the Department of Defense, during the cold war the Seneca Army Depot in Romulus held the largest stockpile of nuclear weapons in the country. The 11,000-acre base was an explosives, chemical weapons, and hazardous material supply depot, with 519 ammunition storage igloos and over 20 large warehouses. Government and corporate negligence led to the disposal of weapons by detonation, incineration, and open burning, and the contents of some dumping areas are still classified by the army. Seneca Army Depot was closed in 2000.

*Factoid*: First discovered by Army personnel after the depot was built in 1941, a herd of rare white deer populate the grounds. A recessive gene for lack of pigmentation apparently prevents usual brown coloration of the hair. The limited predators and controlled hunting on the former Depot have allowed the white deer to interbreed and increase in numbers for more than 60 years. Guided bus tours now take visitors through an area called "Deer Haven Park" to view the rare herd.

## BEETLE MANIA

As a student in the Architecture School at Cornell University, Stephen Gibian used the summer of 1976 to build a life-size Volkswagon Beetle from a pile of fieldstones. He found four rubble boulders for the classic VW fenders. Windows were slabs of stone from a local quarry. The rear license plate was carved from a block of antique sandstone. For the final touch, Gibian scavenged a few vintage VW parts, including hubcaps, bumpers, wipers, and hood insignia. Not a public art installation, the Stone Beetle rests on private property near the intersection of Ringwood Road and Midline Road in Freeville, just north of Ithaca.

*Factoid*: In 1989, architect Stephen Gibian designed the permanent structure that houses the Ithaca Farmers Market at Steamboat Landing with references to historic European public markets.

## MOUNT TRASHMORE

Seneca Falls is the site of Seneca Meadows, the largest landfill in New York State, and one of the largest in the entire northeastern United States, taking in an average of 6,000 tons of garbage and industrial waste every day. The dump accepts trash from New York, Massachusetts, Connecticut, New Jersey and Pennsylvania, and at its peak, the stinking mountain of trash is the highest point for miles around in any direction. Seneca Meadows recycles two million tires a year, making it one of the largest tire recyclers in the country. The tires are chopped up and the chips used in place of stone for drainage. The trash produces methane gas as it decomposes and is then burned to produce electricity, enough to power 15,000 to

18,000 homes. Although detractors complain about the dust, the odors and the thousands of gulls hovering and swooping above the site, tax revenues from Seneca Meadows have paid for many of the region's public improvements.

*Factoid*: In 2007 Seneca Meadows created a 600-acre wetland preserve as part of a mitigation measure to replace wetlands destroyed by expansion of the landfill. The preserve encompasses several open ponds, vast fields of grassland, and a variety of wetland habitats. Several endangered or "vulnerable" species are known to live in the preserve.

## THE LONG AND THE SHORT OF IT

Despite its Native American translation meaning "Long Lake," Canadice Lake is the shortest of the Finger Lakes, measuring just under 4 miles in length. In 1872, the City of Rochester began buying up the properties surrounding the lake in preparation for making it a source of clean drinking water for the city, passing up the closer supply of fresh water from Lake Ontario.

*Factoid*: Canadice, it seems, has a higher elevation than the city, allowing for natural water pressure to build up and decreasing the need for robust pumping equipment.

## ALL'S WELLS THAT ENDS WELLS

Henry Wells began his career as an expressman in upstate New York, delivering trunks filled with small valuables, letters, and funds for an agreed-upon price, at a time when such services were still relatively new in the United States. Wells met another like-minded young man named William Fargo, and the two men combined their operations along with several business rivals to form the American Express Company in March 1850. After gold was discovered in California, Wells and Fargo wanted to branch out from the East Coast, but other partners in American Express refused to expand westward. Wells and Fargo organized a separate company to pursue their strategy, and on March 18, 1852, Wells, Fargo & Co. was born. Wells retired from the board of Wells Fargo in 1867 and retired as president of American Express in 1868, the year he founded Wells College in Aurora, one of the first women's colleges in the United States. After 136 years as a women's college, Wells become a co-educational institution in 2005.

*Factoid*: At age 21, Frances Folsom Cleveland, Wells Class of 1885, became the youngest First Lady of the United States when she married 49-year-old Grover Cleveland. She was the first First Lady to be a college graduate and the only First Lady to be wed in the White House.

## THE DINER PIE

The name of the village was contrived from the first syllables of "Pennsylvania" and "Yankee," as most of the early settlers were Pennsylvanians and New Englanders (or Yankees). When Penn Yan incorporated in 1833, it was already home to five taverns. But it wasn't until 1925 that this Yates County village had its own truly unique American institution, a diner. Built by the Galion Dining Car Company in Galion, Ohio, the trolley-car-shaped Penn Yan Diner was originally purchased by Byron and Lena Legters and installed in a vacant lot east of the Masonic Temple. It's had a succession of owners over the years, and has been operated since 2012 by Carrie and Sean Ahearn.

*Factoid*: The Penn Yan Diner is faithful to the tradition of the diner pie, and with a daily choice of Sean's house-baked fat pies, the best thing you can get your hands on for dessert, especially with a cup of thick black coffee on the side.

# FRIDAY NIGHT FLIGHTS

Wine grapes flourish in the Finger Lakes because of the "microclimate" of the region. Deep lake waters delay the first fall frost – very important to a successful harvest. The term provides the name and theme of Microclimate Wine Bar, an odd little space at 38 Linden Street in Geneva, where you can choose from a range of tasting flights that each pit a Finger Lakes varietal against its counterpart from other wine producing regions, providing a unique opportunity to compare local wines with comparable wines produced worldwide. Microclimate's flights changes every two to three months, except for the Rieslings, which persist because of the importance of this signature variety to the Finger Lakes region.

*Factoid*: The old school definition of "flight" is a collection or grouping of similar objects such as a flight of birds. Flights generally represent a grouping of wines that share some characteristics, and a tasting sampler of more than two wines is called a flight.

## THIS PLACE IS FOR THE BIRDS – LITERALLY

The Cornell Lab of Ornithology in Ithaca, more commonly known as Sapsucker Woods, is a birding haven and resource for both long time bird-watchers and those with aspiring interest. Industrialist Lyman K. Stuart, a 1921 graduate of Cornell, had a lifelong interest in ornithology, and his hobby, photography, won him a *Life* magazine award in 1954 in a national amateur photo essay contest for a study called "Wild Birds in Flight." That same year Stuart purchased farmland which was set aside for the sanctuary and helped finance the construction of the first building in 1957. Lab founder Arthur Allen, along with colleagues Louis Agassiz Fuertes, James Gutsell, and Francis Harper, dubbed the area Sapsucker Woods after discovery of the first breeding yellow-bellied sapsucker ever reported in the Cayuga Lake Basin.

*Factoid*: For visiting birdwatchers, four miles of trails wander through the 230-acres of deep woods, atop boardwalks in swamps, and beside ponds bursting with wildlife of all kinds.

## THE TOWN THAT NEVER WAS

Valentown is the name of a three-story structure near Victor in Ontario County, built in 1879 by Levi and Alanson Valentine and intended as the central commercial and community center of a proposed new town to be created by Valentine and named "Valentown." The Valentine brothers' motive was a forthcoming railroad line that was to travel past the building. However, their forward-thinking plan yielded an unfortunate result when the Pittsburgh, Shawmut, and Northern Railroad went bankrupt and did not complete the line. With no demand for a commercial center in the location, Valentown quickly failed as an enterprise and was abandoned.

*Factoid*: In 1940, local historian J. Sheldon Fisher purchased the structure and created the Valentown Museum, operated today by the Victor Historical Society and the inside remains much as it was when originally built, including a general store, meeting room, bakery, harness shop, cobbler's shop, music school, Grange meeting room, railroad/trolley/telegraph office, ticket office and Grand Ballroom.

## CAR-TOONIST

Road Racing came to Watkins Glen in 1948, initiated by Cameron Argetsinger, a law student at Cornell University in Ithaca. The "Watkins Glen Grand Prix," a 6.6 mile course using mostly paved roads was held at 12 Noon on October 2nd, 1948. Fifteen cars started the 8-lap, 52.8 mile race, and ten finished. The winner was Frank Griswold, of Wayne, Pennsylvania in a pre-war Alfa Romeo 8C2900 coupe, closely followed by Briggs Cunningham in a modified Bu-Merc. Other prominent entrants included

William Milliken, the noted aircraft and race vehicle dynamics expert (who rolled his Bugatti 35 on the last lap, giving "Milliken's Corner" its name). The innocence of Watkins Glen was shattered in 1952, when one of the cars crashed into spectators, killing a seven-year-old boy. That was the end of street racing in Watkins Glen.

*Factoid*: Charles Addams, the cartoonist who created the darkly humorous and macabre characters who became known as the Addams Family, entered his souped-up 220-hp 1927 Mercedes-Benz in that first race wearing a Sherlock Holmes-style deerstalker hat.

## SPACE WALK

Among the most important thinkers of the 20th Century, Carl Sagan popularized astronomy, astrophysics and science, most notably in the award-winning PBS series *Cosmos: A Personal Voyage*, seen by 600 million viewers in over 60 countries. He served as Professor of Astronomy and Director of the Laboratory for Planetary Studies at Cornell University until his death in 1996. Created in his memory, the Carl Sagan Memorial Planet Walk in Ithaca is a series of 11 interactive stone monoliths, each one representing an item in the solar system, distanced throughout the city over the span of three quarters of a mile to an exact 1:5 billion scale of the solar system from the sun at Center Ithaca to Pluto at the Sciencenter. An audio tour for cell phones and media players, narrated by Bill Nye, was added in 2003, and in 2012, the Planet Walk got much longer when – in keeping with the 5-billion-to-1 scale – a station depicting Alpha Centauri, the star nearest the sun, was added at the University of Hawaii campus, making the Planet Walk the largest permanent exhibition in the world.

*Factoid*: The Sciencenter's permanent home at 601 First Street in Ithaca was designed by local architect Bob Leathers and built with over 2,200 Ithacans contributing more than 40,000 hours of work.

# ABNER'S PASTIME

Abner Doubleday spent his childhood in Auburn, then attended a preparatory high school in Cooperstown. He practiced as a surveyor and civil engineer for two years before entering the United States Military Academy in 1838. Legend has it that Doubleday invented the game of baseball, the evolution from a variety of stick-and-ball contests played at the time, with the "first game" allegedly played in Cooperstown on June 12, 1839. Doubleday's true claim to fame lies with his heroics as a Union general in the Civil War. He fired the first shot in defense of Fort Sumter in response to the bombardment by secessionist forces, the opening battle of the war, and had a pivotal role at the Battle of Gettysburg, where he repulsed Confederate fighting under General Robert E. Lee.

*Factoid*: The Class-A affiliate of the Washington Nationals, the Auburn Doubledays, play their home games at the 2,800-seat Falcon Park on North Division Street in Auburn.

# THE ICE MAN COMETH

On March 29, 1867, Russian minister Baron Eduard de Stoeckl and American Secretary of State William Henry Seward (Abraham Lincoln's "right hand man") completed the draft of a treaty ceding Alaska to the United States, and the treaty was signed early the following day. The settlement was $7.2 million – about two cents per acre. Despite the bargain price, the Alaskan purchase was ridiculed in Congress and in the press as "Seward's Folly" or "Seward's Icebox," and newspaper editorials insisted that taxpayer money had been wasted on a "Polar Bear Garden." Born in Florida, New York, Seward inherited a house at 33 South Street in Auburn from his father-in-law, Elijah Miller. Although he spent many years in Albany and Washington, D.C., Seward called this house his home from the time of his marriage in 1824 until his death.

*Factoid*: The home is packed with unexpected bits of history, from Seward's extensive Civil War-era library to a collection of souvenirs from his world travels. These include an Aleutian boat made of animal skins and a gold ring made from the last spike driven in the first transcontinental railroad. The strangest display is the blood-stained sheet left from a bizarre and nearly successful assassination attempt against Seward the same night Lincoln was killed.

## DOUBLE SAWBUCK

Born into slavery in Dorchester County, Maryland, Harriet Tubman escaped to freedom in the North in 1849 to become the most famous "conductor" on the Underground Railroad. She risked her life leading hundreds of other slaves to freedom along an elaborate secret network of safe houses. During the Civil War, Tubman served as a nurse, cook, spy and scout. After the Emancipation Proclamation became the law of the land, she returned to the family home on property she had purchased in 1859 in Auburn, where she dedicated her life to helping impoverished former slaves and the elderly. The Harriet Tubman Home at 180 South Street Road in Auburn is now a National Historic Landmark.

*Factoid*: The $20 bill is often called a "Jackson" or a double sawbuck, since it's twice the value of a ten. In honor of her life and by popular demand, in 2016, the U.S. Treasury Department announced that Harriet Tubman will replace Andrew Jackson on the center of a new $20 bill.

## LONGEST HOME RUN

On April 21, 1923, the Columbia University baseball team arrived in Ithaca to play the Cornell University squad on Hoy Field. That day, a home run walloped by the starting pitcher and powerful left-handed hitter for Columbia remains the farthest ever hit here – according to witnesses, a distance of 450 feet from home plate. The player's name was Henry Louis Gehrig, and later that year, baseball scout Paul Krichell was so impressed with the young man's hitting skills he was offered a $1,500 bonus and a contract with the New York Yankees. Lou Gehrig left Columbia and went on to become one of the greatest and most beloved players in baseball history, hitting a total of 493 home runs over 15 seasons for the Yankees.

*Factoid*: Babe Ruth hit a home run, a triple and a single in an exhibition game at Dunn Field in Elmira on October 17, 1928.

## COUNTER CULTURE

The legendary Ithaca diner on West State Street called Obie's was a domed, railroad car-shaped gathering place with ten seats at the counter and two tables. Obie's claim to fame is the Bo-Burger, a combination devised in the early 1950s for Bo Roberson, Cornell's All-America football star, the only person ever to earn an Ivy League degree, an Olympic medal, and a doctorate, while going on to an NFL career (as wide receiver he was the Oakland Raiders' most valuable player in 1962). The culinary masterpiece consisted of a hamburger topped with finely-diced, sautéed onions, fried egg with a broken yolk, and melted cheese. Bo-Burgers were very good to proprietor Obie, who sold enough of them to buy a new Cadillac every year and vacation every July and August in Spain.

*Factoid*: The Tullyburger (grilled cheeseburger with raw onions, lettuce, tomato and mayonnaise) originated at Wes and Les's, across from the old Lehigh Valley station in Ithaca, its combination inspired by John M. Tully, Cornell Class of '46. (You can still order a Bo-Burger or Tully Burger at the State Diner in Ithaca's West End or at Lincoln Street Diner in the Fall Creek neighborhood).

# WHEN HOPE IS LOST

James Hope was born on November 29, 1819 in Scotland, and after moving to the United States he became a portrait, landscape, and historical genre painter. During the Civil War, he served in the Union army and made on-the-spot sketches, most notably of the bloody battle of Antietam, which he later converted to large paintings exhibited throughout the country. After living much of his life in Vermont, in 1872 he moved to Watkins Glen, where he built a studio and art gallery. There he spent the last twenty years of his life as artist laureate of the geologic formations found in the vicinity, especially Rainbow Falls.

*Factoid:* The Hope Gallery fell into disrepair after his death in 1892, and in the flood of 1935, much of his work, including the battle scene paintings, was damaged or destroyed.

# MYSTERY OF THE BURNING SPRINGS

It was the Native American Senecas who taught French explorer, Robert de LaSalle how to make long journeys overland, on foot in any season, subsisting on game and bags of corn. On his trek across the Finger Lakes in 1669, de LaSalle wrote to his homeland describing a site eight miles from the foot of Canandaigua Lake, where the Senecas had escorted him to see "magical burning water," natural gas bubbling to the surface which had probably been ignited by lightning. The "burning springs" are on what is now Case Road in the Ontario County town of Bristol.

*Factoid*: Natural gas springs were formed from organic material caught in-between layers of mud millions of years ago when the Finger Lakes region was covered by a shallow ocean. The organic material decayed and was subject to intense pressure, forming natural gas, which became trapped within layers of shale rock. The gas rises through fissures in the slate.

# THE PARK PARK

In 1942, at the behest of the Grange League Federation, a farmer-owned cooperative, Roy H. Park established an advertising agency in Ithaca. The firm was engaged to find a trademark name under which the cooperative could sell their food products, and Park went after the top name in eating – Duncan Hines, famed for his guidebooks and signs recommending top restaurants nationwide. Premium-priced Duncan Hines Cake Mix was the first product, and it soon vaulted to number one on the nation's grocery shelves. (The Duncan Hines world headquarters and test kitchen was established at 408 East State Street in Ithaca, now a 10-room boutique hotel call the Argos Inn). After Procter & Gamble purchased the company in 1956, Park began a second career in communications. Starting in 1962, he acquired or built 22 radio stations, 11 television stations, and 144 publications, including 41 daily newspapers in 24 states. In 1966, he created the Park Foundation, which has funded many programs in his name at Ithaca College, Cornell University, and North Carolina State University. In Ithaca, the foundation has provided funding for one of the country's first no-kill animal shelters, the Ithaca Free Clinic, a new headquarters for the Tompkins County Library, a new organ for the First Presbyterian Church, and a merry-go-round at Stewart Park.

*Factoid*: In 1998, the Park Foundation gifted the "Park Park," a protected natural area situated on either side of Forest Home Drive in Ithaca, near the intersection of Route 366. A one-quarter mile spur trail crosses Forest Home Drive to a scenic picnic area with stone tables on the banks of Fall Creek and winds through a variety of plant communities including forest, shrub thicket, wetland, meadow and prairie near Fall Creek.

# JETHRO'S FOLLY

Jethro Wood was a blacksmith from Scipio in Cayuga County, credited with the invention of a light, strong cast iron plow whose parts were held together by lugs and locking pieces. It was the first plow in which the parts most exposed to wear could be replaced in the field with new parts. (During the development of his plow, Wood corresponded with Thomas Jefferson, who had been working on an improvement to the plow along slightly different lines). Wood received a patent for an initial version of his cast-iron plow in 1814, with additionally patented improvements on that plow in 1819. He began to manufacture his plows, spending a large part of his fortune in the process. However, his neighbors called the device "Jethro's Folly," and all agreed that it would never work. Actually, it did work, and as the first commercially successful iron moldboard plow, his invention accelerated the development of American agriculture during the period.

*Factoid*: After the invention of the plow, much of Wood's time and money were consumed by pursuing patent infringement suits against small manufacturers around the country who had copied his design. Wood died in poverty in 1834.

## THE LADY IN GRANITE

Born in 1959, Matilda Bishop married Francis Gillette, cousin of King C. Gillette, inventor of the safety razor. After her death in 1936, she was buried in Lakeview Cemetery in Penn Yan, where her granite headstone inexplicably formed a large white irregular shape thought to resemble the woman's profile on her deathbed, or in her coffin. The image is a milky white blob about fourteen inches long and six inches wide under the highly polished surface in the dark granite, on the south side of the monument. Accounts of her marriage vary, but many claim she had a troubled relation-ship with her husband and vowed to haunt him after she passed.

*Factoid*: Frank Swann, Yates County Historian, declared the so-called "face" was simply a blemish in the granite. The proprietor of a local monument company confirmed the image was caused by a flaw in the granite that became more apparent after years of weathering. No amount of polishing has ever been able to remove it. (As one enters Lakeview Cemetery by the Lake Street entrance, the monument is located a short distance up the hill on the left side of the second road to the right).

## PASS THE LOBSTER NEWBURG

A Skaneateles building that dates to the 1830s became a restaurant in 1899 when Fred and Cora Krebs began serving meals to neighbors. The Krebs enjoyed many years of success as a dining destination along Route 20, hosting notable visitors including Franklin D. Roosevelt (when he was governor), John Barrymore, Maxie Rosenbloom, Grace Moore, and more recently, Bill and Hillary Clinton. Traditional and highly ritualized seven-course dinners included Lobster Newburg for which the restaurant became famous. During its glory years, the restaurant served eight hundred meals a day on average, with twelve hundred to fifteen hundred on Saturdays and Sundays. The Krebs passed through three generations of the Krebs family before it was sold to scrap metal tycoon Adam Weitsman.

*Factoid*: Under the Weitzman ownership, the Krebs donates all of net profits to charitable organizations and non-profits benefiting women and children throughout Central New York.

## THOMAS EDISON OF POULTRY

In the late 1950s, Robert C. Baker, Cornell professor of food science, began developing more ways to use chicken and eggs. He believed that consumers would eat more if they had more convenient alternatives, and he went on to invent 50 edible products from eggs and chicken, but made to look like something else. Baker's marinade for barbecued chicken, known as "Cornell Chicken," has become a regional staple at roadside stands, firefighter fund-raisers, and company picnics throughout the Finger Lakes. The marinade is sold in regional groceries as "Salamida Original State Fair Famous Cornell-Style Chicken Bar-B-Que Sauce."

*Factoid*: Credit (or blame) for McDonald's Chicken McNuggets goes to Mr. Baker, whose unpatented innovation made it possible to form chicken pieces into any shape.

## THE MUSEUM THAT FLOOR WAX BUILT

In 1886, Samuel Curtis Johnson formulated a product to care for parquet floors, and 87 years later his grandson, Herbert Fisk Johnson, Jr., became the primary benefactor of the art museum perched atop a 1,000-foot slope on the northwest corner of the Arts Quad of the Cornell University campus in Ithaca. Designed by architect I. M. Pei, the massive reinforced concrete form has been compared to a sewing machine, a piano, even a giraffe.

*Factoid*: The museum was built on the very spot where Ezra Cornell stood when he announced his intention to found the university, in opposition to the wishes of Andrew Dickson White, the university's co-founder and first president, who insisted that no building be constructed on this hallowed ground. Pei called his desire to build on the site "an obsession."

## THE OTHER WILL SMITH

Not the actor/rapper who once called himself "The Fresh Prince," another William Smith arrived in Geneva from England in 1843 at the age of 25, began raising and selling ornamental plants, and accumulated a sizeable fortune. He built the magnificent, Romanesque-style Smith Opera House which opened on October 29, 1894 with a production of *The Count of Monte Cristo*, starring James O'Neill, father of playwright Eugene O'Neill. The Smith continues as one of the oldest operating performing arts theaters in the United States. It is recognized by the National Register of Historic Places and has been called an architectural gem by *The New York Times* and the Smithsonian.

*Factoid*: To make ends meet, a struggling musician named Bruce Springsteen toured constantly in between recording sessions for the "Born to Run" album. Springsteen arrived in Geneva along with members of the E Street Band to perform at the Smith on December 7, 1974.

## THE CHERRY ON TOP

In 1892, the soda fountain menu at Platt & Colt Pharmacy on State Street in Ithaca offered a dish of ice cream for a nickel, and local Unitarian minister John M. Scott often stopped in after Sunday services for a scoop of vanilla. One visit in particular proved memorable. On a whim, proprietor Chester C. Platt dipped Reverend Scott's ice cream into a champagne saucer, poured cherry syrup over the top, and dressed it with a candied cherry. As the two men pondered over what to call the new concoction, Scott proposed that it be named "Ice Cream Sunday" after the day it was invented. By the turn-of-the-century (and with a change in spelling that distinguished the dessert from the Sabbath), ice cream sundaes were being served nationwide.

*Factoid*: Although several other cities challenge Ithaca's claim as birthplace of the sundae, an *Ithaca Journal* advertisement for Platt & Colt dated May 28, 1892, provides irrefutable evidence. The ad promotes the fountain's "Cherry Sunday" as "a new ten-cent specialty."

## All Aboard!

Besides seventeen conventional rooms, the Caboose Motel on Route 415 in Avoca features five 1916-era cabooses, restored and converted into guest rooms. Each railroad car is equipped with a bathroom and shower, seating, cable TV, telephone, two upper berths (original sleepers), one single and one double bed for lower berths. Each room has a volume-controlled speaker that simulates the sound of a train in motion.

*Factoid*: Intended to provide shelter for the crew who kept a lookout from the windowed cupola for load shifting, damage to cargo, and over-heating axles, cabooses were used on every freight train until the 1980s, when safety laws requiring the presence of cabooses and full crews were relaxed.

## IMPRESSIONIST INDULGENCE

Near his home in Giverny, France, Claude Monet re-channeled a small creek to supply a pond for growing aquatic plants. Then he erected a foot-bridge modeled after a Japanese print and covered it with blue and white wisteria. The exotic water garden with its meditative water lilies became the subject of many of the most beloved paintings by the great French im-pressionist. On a dozen wooded acres just outside the village of Skaneate-les, Linda Dal Pos, an interior designer, and Gary Dower, a shopping mall developer, have reproduced a serene French country estate called Mirbeau Inn & Spa, with pale yellow guest cottages, enclosed gardens, and lily ponds straight out of a Monet canvass. Guest rooms include fireplaces, over-sized bathrooms with walk-in showers, soaking tubs, double sinks, and plush mattresses. The full-service spa offers a selection of wraps, massages, facials, and mineral baths.

*Factoid*: The waterlilies at Mirbeau were sourced from Latour-Marliac, the same nursery where Monet bought his plants.

## NABOKOV'S NYMPHET

Vladimir Nabokov's novel *Lolita* has been called both "the filthiest book ever written" and "the best book ever written." Nabokov came to

Ithaca in 1948 to teach Russian Literature at Cornell University at the urging of Morris Bishop, Professor of Romance Literature and University Historian. After just a few months in a small apartment at 957 East State Street, Nabokov and his family moved into more comfortable quarters at 802 East Seneca Street. It was primarily at these two homes where he wrote *Lolita*, the story of a middle-aged professor's obsession with a sexually precocious 12-year-old girl. Within a year after the debut of *Lolita* in 1958, Nabokov left Ithaca. He had earned enough money from the book that he could afford to stop teaching and write full-time, and he spent the rest of his life in Montreux, Switzerland. *Lolita* has sold 50 million copies.

*Factoid*: According to Nabokov's biographer Brian Boyd, to get the details of his central character right "he would do things like travel on the buses around Ithaca and record phrases, in a little notebook, from young girls that he heard coming back from school."

## *MOVEABLE MIXOLOGIST*

Not long after a visit by prohibitionist Carrie Nation and her famous hatchet, the town of Elmira went dry, a full four years before the Eighteenth Amendment became the law of the land. At the time, Edward J. Weaver, owner of the Weaver Hotel, continued to sell alcoholic beverages, claiming his hotel to be in neighboring town of Big Flats. After a survey showed the hotel to be straddling the town line, Weaver put his mahogany bar on casters, and it was pushed from the dry town side of the hotel to the wet town side, keeping his establishment in compliance with local law.

*Factoid*: The Weaver Hotel was "the country club" of its time where prominent men came to play cards. The hotel had 17 overnight guest rooms and a dance hall on the second floor.

# CABBAGE PATCH

The sauerkraut industry in the Ontario County town of Phelps evolved around the turn of the last century, attracted by the concentration of cabbage growers who enjoyed the ideal cool, rainy growing seasons of the area. Since cabbage is a weighty, low☐value item, it didn't pay to ship it far for processing, and with the opening of the Silver Floss factory in 1900, Phelps became known as "the sauerkraut capital of the world," producing more than a third of more than 300 million pounds of sauerkraut, consumed annually in this country. But canning in Phelps ended in 1985 as Silver Floss moved production to Shortsville at a factory operated by GLK Foods, a company with roots back to a Wisconsin cannery that started making sauerkraut in 1900. Then in 2018, GLK moved all production to Wisconsin.

*Factoid*: Local sauerkraut is gone, but the annual Phelps Sauerkraut Festival goes on. Since 1967, the festival has featured "everything sauerkraut," from Reuben sandwiches to sauerkraut beer made by a local brewery, and each year the Sauerkraut Festival Prince and Princess cut a sauerkraut cake. The Phelps Sauerkraut Weekend 20K is the second oldest footrace in New York State.

# GEORGIA ON MY MIND

McGregor Vineyard, perched high above Keuka Lake in Dundee, makes its mark on Finger Lakes viticulture with plantings of rare, Eastern-European wine grapes, propagated from a mother lode of cuttings that originated in the former Soviet Republic of Georgia. Two hardy varieties with noble bloodlines, Saperavi and Sereksia Charni, are married to produce an audacious red blend called "Black Russian."

*Factoid*: Even more obscure than Saperavi, Sereksia Charni and is grown around the Black and Caspian Seas in Ukraine, Armenia, and

Romania. McGregor is the only producer of a wine from this grape variety in the Western Hemisphere.

# *Burger Meister*

Glenwood Pines traces its history to the days just after World War II when the spot on Route 89 north of Ithaca was occupied by a cinder block stand selling fresh produce and ice cream. The stand was sold to Harry and Frances Dearstyne in 1951, who enlarged the building and added a small lunch menu. By the time Elmer and Lou Morgan bought the Glenwood in 1962, it was a full-scale restaurant. The legendary Pinesburger made its debut under owners Lee Denman and Dave Pepin in the 1970s. Each grilled one-third-pound cheeseburger with mayo or Thousand Island dressing, is generously adorned with lettuce, tomato, and onions, and served on a miniloaf of fresh French bread baked at the local Ithaca Bakery.

*Factoid*: Anyone who eats four Pinesburgers in less than one hour receives a souvenir bobblehead.

# HORSE THIEVES AND NO-GOODERS

The Central Exchange Hotel, a stop on routes from Elmira to Auburn and Cortland to Penn Yan, where stage coaches exchanged horses, was built in 1830 by General Daniel Minier in what was then known as Libertyville (now South Lansing). It cost $40,000 to build and took 12 years to complete. It features 15-inch-thick brick walls and 13 working fire places. The first known bill for the hotel was "50 cents admission, supper and horses extra." William Miller, a later owner, renamed it the Elm Grove Hotel in 1890 for the row of elm trees planted in front of the inn. By the turn of the century, Rogues Harbor began to attract a clientele locals described as "horse thieves and no-gooders."

*Factoid*: Rogues Harbor received its current name when it is said that a patron in high spirits climbed to the roof of a nearby building, and hurling a bottle of whiskey against the brick, proposed a toast, "here's to a harbor of rogues."

## POLAR BEAR PLUNGE

In the early 1800s it was called the Keuka Hotel, and after purchase by the Switzer family in 1894, renamed the Switzerland Inn. The old girl hugging the eastern shore of Keuka Lake now shows her age in places, but under the current ownership of Joshua Trombley, the Switz has earned local landmark status for genial service and dependable food and drink. When you visit, be sure to say hello to "Marty, the One Man Party," a regular at the Switz bar.

*Factoid*: In longstanding tradition, the Switz plays host to the annual Polar Bear Plunge. Each year on the last Saturday of March, dozens of participants hurl themselves off the dock into Keuka Lake's chilly waters. Prizes are awarded for Most Original Costume and Oldest Jumper.

## ROCKS AND FOSSILS

It all began with a dispute over the safety of his fossil collection. Gilbert D. Harris, a Cornell University professor from 1894 to 1934, was nearing retirement and intended to leave thousands of priceless fossils and research papers to the university, on condition that the geology department provide a secure fire-proof building with nonflammable furnishings. When Cornell failed to comply, Harris packed up the collection and took it home – literally. He built his own facility of concrete, with metal fixtures, next to his home in Ithaca's Cayuga Heights neighborhood. It was the beginning of the Paleontological Research Institution, chartered as an independent educational institution by the state of New York in 1933.

*Factoid*: In 1968 PRI moved across the lake to 1259 Trumansburg

Road, a facility now housing one of the largest collections of invertebrate fossils in North America, including classic Devonian aged (416 to 359 million years old) rocks of the Finger Lakes region.

## Traffic "Jam"

An estimated 600,000 rock fans showed up for the Summer Jam outside Watkins Glen on July 28, 1973, to see the Allman Brothers Band, Grateful Dead and The Band perform on the Grand Prix Raceway grounds. Four years after the legendary Woodstock concert, fans who had attended Woodstock – or regretted missing it – came looking for a repeat of music and a freewheeling party. An enormous a 100-mile long traffic jam created impassable roads and overwhelmed public services. For days, Watkins Glen, Montour Falls and other nearby hamlets were without police and fire protection, mail service, and even food deliveries because of clogged roads. Traffic backed up on the Thruway at Geneva, Routes 14 and 414. With traffic stopped and concert time getting closer, fans simply abandoned cars and walked. A week after the concert, police were still dealing with abandoned vehicles. Often owners had forgotten where they parked.

*Factoid*: Historians claimed that the Watkins Glen event was the largest gathering of people in the history of the United States. On that July 28, one out of every 350 people living in America at the time was listening to the sounds of rock at the Watkins Glen racetrack grounds.

## Keepers of the Paddle

Generations of Hobart College members of the Druid Society have preserved the legend of Seneca Indian warrior Agayentah (*Ah-gay-EN-tah*), who after seeking refuge under a tree during a thunderstorm, was struck by lightning and killed instantly. Both warrior and tree were swept into the stormy waters of Seneca Lake. Around 1840, a Hobart student claimed to have found the paddle from Agayentah's canoe, and the paddle was handed down by the outgoing Druids to their successors at what is now Hobart's Charter Day.

*Factoid*: An annual event initiated in 2004 officially welcomes soon-to-be Hobart graduates into the Alumni Association. Each member of the class is given a replica of the paddle used by Agayentah, symbolically intended to navigate their lives through stormy weather.

## YOU ARE WHAT YOU EAT

Mothership of the legendary vegetarian cookbook, Moosewood restaurant at 215 North Cayuga Street in Ithaca is anchored in a school-building-turned-alternative-mall, where for forty-some years they have been serving meat-free comfort food minus the sanctimony. Founded by seven original members in 1973, Moosewood became a wellspring for a number of vegetarian cookbooks, but not without controversy. The original *Moosewood Cookbook* by Molly Katzen included pen-and-ink illustrations and hand-lettered recipes she claims were developed without participation of the restaurant collective. First produced in an un-bylined, spiral-bound booklet, it was discovered by Philip Wood of then-fledgeling Ten Speed Press who first recognized the potential of a groundbreaking vegetarian cookbook. Katzen's association with the restaurant had long since lapsed when Wood signed Katzen to a contract that excluded members of the group from receiving any royalties, as well as prohibiting publication of their own books using the Moosewood name, for a period of several years. Katzen's *Moosewood Cookbook* went on to become one of the best-selling cookbooks of all time. Since the restriction was lifted, the Moosewood collective has produced a series of its own cookbooks.

*Factoid*: *Bon Appetit* magazine named Moosewood as one of the most influential restaurants of the twentieth century, at the forefront of a movement that has had a profound impact on the American diet.

# ICE SKATING ACROSS CAYUGA

The longest of the Finger Lakes at nearly 40 miles, Cayuga measures 435 feet at its deepest point. Its average width is 1.7 miles, and 3.5 miles wide at its widest point near Aurora. Its depth, steep east and west sides with shallow north and south ends is typical of the Finger Lakes, carved by glaciers during the last ice age. During six weeks of excessive cold in the winter of 1912, ice twenty-two to twenty-four inches thick formed in the shallows at both ends of the lake, and as the cold weather continued, the frozen area gradually extended outward. During the night of February 10, the wind subsided, and the morning of the 11th found Cayuga Lake frozen from end to end.

*Factoid*: A well-documented Wells College tradition holds that when the lake freezes over, the college president declares a school holiday. With classes canceled in 1875, student Emma Lampert skated across Cayuga Lake and back.

# BLACK TROOPS IN UNION BLUE

The National Cemetery in the Steuben County town of Bath includes 72 African Civil War veterans whose headstones bear the designation "USCT," designating members of the United States Colored Troops, men who were eager to enlist in the Union Army and join the fight against slavery. Black soldiers believed that military service would allow them to be seen as equals and prove their right to equality. By the end of that war in April 1865, the 175 USCT regiments had constituted about one-tenth of the manpower of the Union Army. About 20 per cent of USCT soldiers died, a rate 35 per cent higher than that for white Union troops. Despite heavy casualties, many fought with distinction, with 15 USCT receiving the Medal of Honor.

*Factoid*: The motion picture *Glory*, starring Denzel Washington who portrayed African-American USCT soldiers of the Massachusetts Volunteer Infantry Regiment.

## *RUSH TO JUDGEMENT*

The town of Rush in the northwestern corner of the Finger Lakes region was founded in 1818 and named either for Dr. Benjamin Rush, Surgeon General to the Continental Army during the American Revolution, a member of the first Continental Congress, and a signer of the Declaration of Independence, or named for his son, Richard Rush, an American states-man and diplomat who served as attorney general in President James Madison's administration. To date, no documentation has been discovered to clearly identify which of these theories might be the actual namesake.

*Factoid*: Rush is the home of Gary Lewis, son of legendary comedian Jerry Lewis, and leader of the 1960s-era pop group Gary Lewis and the Playboys.

## *FOR WHOM THE BELLS TOLL*

McGraw Tower on the campus of Cornell University in Ithaca houses the oldest continuously played set of chimes on an American college cam-pus, marking the hours and chiming concerts since the original set of bells first rang at the university's opening ceremonies on October 7, 1868. One of Cornell's most-beloved traditions, the chimes are played by student chimemasters, three or more 15-minute concerts a day during the school year (with a reduced number of performances when classes are not in session). Morning concerts include the "Jennie McGraw Rag," a carillon classic, christened in honor of the donor. Midday concerts conclude with the Cornell alma mater.

*Factoid*: On October 8, 1997, an astonishing, 60-pound pumpkin appeared atop the 173-foot tower, speared through the lightning rod at its apex, and remaining on the lofty perch for most of the following winter. The mystery and sheer daring of the prank generated coverage by the national news media, beginning with an article in *The New York Times* on October 27. No one has ever come forward with information about the identity of the perpetrator or the method of his madness. The pumpkin remained on the tower until it was removed with a crane on March 13, 1998.

## THERE IS A TAVERN IN THE TOWN

Hammondsport is a throwback to a more gentle time in American life, a setting out of a Norman Rockwell painting. There's a pavilion bandstand in the middle of Pulteney Square, and the village green is surrounded by a drugstore, ice cream parlor, post office, and the Village Tavern, the latest in a succession of notable watering holes to roost at the corner of Mechanic and William Streets. The place is flush with great characters and stories dating back to the early 1900s when Pietro "Pete" Grimaldi opened the original beer parlor on this spot. Today the Village Tavern is a central gathering place for area winemakers and other visitors seeking comfort food and local wines.

*Factoid*: Careful not to drop the wine list on your foot, as you could really hurt yourself. A visit to the Village Tavern provides an opportunity to browse through the encyclopedic, 19-page, all-Finger Lakes wine list, novel for both its breadth and entertainment value.

## PRIMAL ROOTS

In 1825, the Reverend William W. Bostwick moved from Albany to Hammondsport and organized the Episcopal Church Society. Bostwick lacked a source of sacramental wine, so he made cuttings from the few vines planted by the owner of the local tavern, Richard Sheffield, who had brought rootstock of several varieties of grapes from the Hudson River region to Hammondsport a few years earlier. Envisioning agricultural development on the barren hillsides where forests once stood, Bostwick encouraged neighbors to plant clippings from the few Isabella and Catawba vines he was growing in his rectory garden. And by 1836, Josiah W. Prentiss, who had obtained cuttings from Bostwick's grapevines, became the first commercial winemaker in New York State.

*Factoid*: The Pleasant Valley Wine Company is now home to the Great Western, Gold Seal, and Widmer brands, once mighty giants in the wine industry. A 25-minute tour includes a bus ride to the original 1860 Great Western facility (Bonded Winery No. 1) and a display of artifacts from early winemaking in the region. Even the wines are museum pieces, most made with native variety grapes, now out of favor as drinkers become more sophisticated in their taste preferences.

## GRATEFUL MOMENT

From the band's inception, the Grateful Dead toured practically non-stop, and in as many as 2,300 performances over their 30-year career, they never played the same set twice. For that matter, they never played a song the same way twice, instead relaxing traditional song structure in order to allow for extended improvisational jams. According to legend, it never worked better than on the night of May 8, 1977 in Barton Hall on the Cornell University campus. That concert is widely regarded by many to be the best single gig the band ever played, and in 2011, a recording of the concert was one of 25 recordings selected that year for preservation in the National Recording Registry at the Library of Congress.

*Factoid*: Built in 1914 and 1915 and originally designed as a drill hall for the Department of Military Science, Barton Hall functioned as an airplane hangar during World War I and served the ROTC as an armory during World War II. It was home to Cornell basketball games from 1919 to 1990 and continues to serve as the home of the Cornell indoor track team. In the days prior to online course registration, students registered for classes in Barton Hall at the start of each semester.

## A TOWN CALLED FARMER

First settled in the late 1790s and early 1800s, the Seneca County village was home to many families from the New England and New Jersey areas. Early businesses included hotels, blacksmiths, post office, bank, and railroad station. All intended to support the local families and the farmers from the surrounding area, the village was first called Farmerville, then Farmer. In 1904, with the increase in summer travelers coming to the area on the Lehigh Valley Railroad, there was a movement to rename the railroad depot to something other than Farmer. The railroad sponsored a contest to suggest names for the station and a school teacher, Georgiana Wheeler, suggested "Interlaken," inspired by her travels to Switzerland.

*Factoid*: As of the most recent census, there were 602 people residing in the village of Interlaken.

## TOMBOY OF THE AIR

Blanche Stuart Scott was born on April 8, 1884, in Rochester. In 1910, Scott became the second woman, after Alice Huyler Ramsey, to drive an automobile across the United States and the first driving westwards from New York City to San Francisco. The publicity surrounding her automobile journey brought her to the attention of Glenn Curtiss who agreed to provide her with flying lessons in Hammondsport, the only woman to receive instruction directly from Curtiss. Scott subsequently became a professional pilot, and the first woman to fly at a public event in America. Her exhibition flying earned the nickname "Tomboy of the Air."

*Factoid*: Scott became an accomplished stunt pilot known for flying upside down and performing "death dives" from an altitude of 4000 feet, then suddenly pulling up only 200 feet from the ground.

## DOLLHOUSES FOR GROWNUPS

A place called Karenville, eight miles from Ithaca, isn't on any map. But at 371 Curtis Road, just off Danby Road, you'll discover an off-grid village of tiny Victorian-inspired houses. Built by Karen Thurnheer on a diminutive scale, the dwellings, no larger than 8 x 12 feet, harken back to a simpler time before electricity and indoor plumbing.

*Factoid*: In order to take a shower, guests, many of whom find Karenville on AirBnB, must first source their water from rain barrels or a well, heat it on the wood stove in the general store, then pour it into the outdoor shower bucket. One bucket equals a 4-to-5-minute shower.

## *GENTLEMANLY GENTLEMAN*

He was known on Capitol Hill as "the gentlemanly gentleman from Massachusetts." After serving three terms as governor and four terms in the U.S. Senate, Leverett Saltonstall stepped down from public service to become a gentleman farmer in the Finger Lakes. His oldest son, also named Leverett, eschewed politics and, instead, distinguished himself in agriculture as professor of agronomy at Cornell, cattle rancher, and seed producer on the 700-acre Treleaven Farm in King Ferry, bordering the eastern shore of Cayuga Lake.

*Factoid*: One parcel of the original estate remains in the Saltonstall family, and, on a pasture where beef cattle once roamed, 27 acres of wine grapes now flourish. Under the Treleaven brand, the Saltonstalls have been producing wines since 1988. The flagship varietal is Chardonnay.

# WHAT LIES BENEATH

One of the natural wonders of Cayuga Lake is invisible to the eye. Deep under the lake is the deepest salt mine in North America (2,300 feet below the surface), a thick salt reserve deposited over 350 million years ago from the evaporating of the ancient inland sea which covered the region. Salt mining began at the south end of Cayuga Lake in 1915, when John Clute organized the Rock Salt Corporation on Portland Point in Lansing, working from a shaft sunk to 1,500 feet. In 1921, Frank Bolton and John Shannon bought the mine and further sank the shaft to 2,000 feet. Cargill, the world's largest privately-owned corporation, acquired the Cayuga mine in 1970 and annually extracts 2 million tons of salt for road deicing, shipped to more than 1,500 highway departments throughout New York and the northeast United States.

*Factoid*: Mineral rights beneath the lake are owned by New York State, but some of the mine extends under privately owned land in the Town of Lansing.

# TENNIS ANYONE?

Luther Sage Kelly was born in Geneva on July 27, 1849. He joined the army at the close of the Civil War, spending three years at outposts in Minnesota and Dakota. At the conclusion of his enlistment, he headed west to the Upper Missouri and Yellowstone River valley where, known as "Yellowstone Kelly," he became one of the most notable hunters, trappers, and Indian scouts of the American West. Among those he encountered in his travels was Sitting Bull, famous leader of the Lakotas. In his later years, Kelly became a friend of Teddy Roosevelt and valued member of the President's Tennis Cabinet.

*Factoid*: The "Tennis Cabinet" began early in Roosevelt's presidency as a group of men who, as the name would suggest, played tennis with the president in the afternoons. The daily tennis sessions were eventually replaced by what Roosevelt called "rough, cross-country walks," obstacle courses whose main goal was to push each man close to his physical limit.

## VILLAGE OF THE DAMNED

Between 1989 and 1989, a series of blood-chilling crimes in the small village of Dryden, just north of Ithaca, earned the town a story in the *National Enquirer* called "Village of the Damned." In the first tragedy, Warren and Delores Harris and their two young children were slain in their home just before Christmas 1989. Dryden football coach Steve Starr was shot to death defending his daughter from an ex-boyfriend in 1994. And in 1996, 16-year-old Dryden High cheerleaders Sarah Haney and Jennifer Bolduc were abducted, murdered, and dismembered. Police found their remains scattered throughout different locations in Chenango County.

*Factoid*: After Investigation Discovery's 5-part TV documentary series explored the brutal deaths in 2017, more than 3,400 residents petitioned the cable channel to stop the limited series (also called *Village of the Damned*) which the petition authors viewed as "voyeurism of human suffering and tragedy."

## HOME OF FRIES AND GRAVY

The owner, it seems, couldn't make up his mind if this was a diner or a restaurant, so he called it a "dinerant." An Auburn landmark, Hunter's Dinerant is a 1951 stainless-steel Jerry O'Mahony-build dining car that replaced a Ward & Dickinson model. It sits precariously cantilevered over Owasco Creek on Genesee Street, the main business route through the city. The cotton-candy pink interior has classic diner detailing at its finest – stainless steel, chrome, formica, and ceramic tile. Local dishes include French fries smothered in gravy and Fretta, a dish of sausage, peppers, onions, ham, and potatoes fried on the griddle then scrambled with eggs.

*Factoid*: Former Vice President Joe Biden's first wife, Neilia, was the daughter of Bob Hunter, the diner's founder. Mrs. Biden was killed in an automobile accident on December 18, 1972.

## TURNCOAT

Saguwatha, a Seneca Indian orator who spoke for the rights of his people, was called "Red Jacket" because of the colorful uniform jacket given him by the British troops during the American Revolution. He allied with the British both because of their long trading relationships and in the hope that they would limit colonial encroachment on Seneca territory. After the British defeat, the Senecas were forced to cede much of their territory to the United States, and Red Jacket switched sides. He led a delegation of Native American leaders to Philadelphia, where President George Washington presented him with a "peace medal." Red Jacket wore this medal on his chest in every portrait painted of him.

*Factoid*: Red Jacket's name inspired an apple orchard, originally planted along the rolling hills of Seneca Lake in 1917. Today, Red Jacket Orchards at 957 Routes 5 & 20 in Geneva grows sixteen varieties of apples, four varieties of strawberries, as well as sweet and sour cherries, rhubarb, peaches, plums, and apricots.

## PET PROJECT

The Tompkins County SPCA was incorporated in Ithaca on February 6, 1901, to prevent carriage horse abuse in the days be-fore automobiles. In 1904, the organization acquired sheltering facilities and took over as pound master for some of the municipalities within the county. For much of its history, the local SPCA has provided sheltering for unwanted dogs and cats, often forced to humanely euthanize animals due to the large volume of homeless pets in the county. The "No Kill" movement, launched in San Francisco in 1994, was embraced by Tompkins County on June 11, 2001, and transitioned over a two-year period to a No-Kill facility.

*Factoid*: Ithaca was the first and, to date, remains one of the only "No Kill, Open Admission" companion animal shelter, never euthanizing healthy, treatable animals while never turning away strays or surrendered pets. *Animal People*, a prominent national journal on animal issues, ranked Ithaca the safest community for companion animals in the United States.

## WINE LEGEND

A Ukrainian-born doctor of enology, Konstantin Frank immigrated to New York in 1951, after having successfully nurtured wine-producing vines through some of Odessa's nastiest winters. His intuitive, imaginative belief that the same vinifera plantings could do no worse in upstate New York vineyards initially fell on deaf ears. He was correct, of course, but it was not until he met Charles Fournier, wine master of Gold Seal Vineyards, that he would be given the opportunity to prove it. The two men collaborated on an experimental Pinot Noir vineyard near Hammondsport, and, heady with success, Dr. Frank established his own winery here in 1962 and proved to the world that European vines could be grown in the region. Fred Frank is now entrusted to preserve the historical accomplishments of his grandfather, Konstantin, who is credited with changing the course of winegrowing in the Finger Lakes.

*Factoid*: *Wine Report* named Dr. Frank Cellars of Hammondsport the "Greatest Wine Producer in the Northeast," and the Dr. Frank tasting room at 9749 Middle Road in Hammondsport was named one of the top ten tasting rooms in America by *USA Today*.

# THE BEATEN PATH

The Finger Lakes Trail is a 950-mile-long footpath, running from the Pennsylvania-New York border in Allegany State Park to the Long Path in the Catskill Forest Preserve. The main FLT crosses through many New York state parks, state forests and wildlife management areas. The network of trails also crosses through the only national forest in New York State and over an additional 400 private landowner properties. The highest elevation on the entire FLT is 3660 feet near Balsam Lake Mountain in the Catskills. The lowest elevation is 430 feet where the trail crosses the Cayuga Inlet near Ithaca.

*Factoid*: Joe Dabes of Dryden (called "Java Joe" for his conspicuous consumption of coffee) has hiked the entire trail ten times.

# MISTPOUFFERS

The occasional sounds of cannon or sonic booms heard around Cayuga Lake are known as "mistpouffers." The phantom thunder is heard on days when there are no storms in the vicinity that could produce thunder and no other obvious source. Sometimes it's accompanied by a rumble that can be felt strongly enough to shake plates and hanging pictures; other times no vibration is felt. The lake seems to be speaking to the surrounding hills, which send back the echoes of its voice in reply. Native Indians believed the booms were the sound of the Great Spirit continuing his work of shaping the earth. Modern theory suggests the noise is caused by natural gas being released from fissures in the rocks at the bottom of the lake. Another term for mistpouffers is "Seneca Guns," originating in Seneca, Georgia, during the Civil War when the rumble of artillery fire could be felt for a distance of up to five miles from the battlefield.

*Factoid*: A similar phenomenon is known to occur near the banks of the river Ganges in India, as well as areas of the North Sea, Japan and Italy.

# BRIDGE TO NOWHERE

It's said that the blue pedestrian bridge built over a four-lane section of Route 13 near Buttermilk Falls in Ithaca is the perfect metaphor for the city's central isolation. Intended to connect proposed trails on each side of the highway, the "Welcome to Ithaca" bridge was built before any rights to the abandoned Delaware, Lackawanna & Western Railroad bed were secured. Widely criticized as a spectacularly visible example of a "pork barrel" waste of tax money, $250,000 of the $365,000 it cost to build the bridge in 2001 was covered by a state grant. Each end of the bridge is sealed off by a chain-link fence, and it's uncertain if the bridge will ever be used as intended.

*Factoid*: The original "Bridge to Nowhere" was a proposed $398,000,000 bridge to replace the ferry that connects the town of Ketchikan, Alaska with Gravina Island, an island with only 50 residents.

# THEY DIDN'T GET HIS GOAT

Walter Taylor, founder of Bully Hill Vineyards in Hammondsport, was a larger-than-life character in the sweeping epic of Finger Lakes wine country. The grandson of the founder of the Taylor Wine Company and an eager provocateur, Walter railed against the "wine factory" the family company had become by the time it was swallowed up by Coca-Cola in 1977. Coca-Cola wasted no time in going after Walter. In short order, a federal court judge enjoined him from using the Taylor name on any of his wines. Walter responded by designing a label bearing his drawing of a goat and the slogan: "They Have My Name and My Heritage, but They Didn't Get My Goat." His great, great, great grandfather, Eliceum Taylor, was a first cousin of P.T. Barnum – Phineas Taylor Barnum – perhaps explaining the showman in Walter.

*Factoid*: A wine museum on the grounds of Bully Hill is devoted to the

Taylor family endeavor that began in 1878.  The Cooper Shop Building includes local memorabilia and wine making equipment from the early days of the Finger Lakes wine industry.  The Art Gallery houses original artwork by Walter, artifacts from the days of Prohibition, presidential glassware, and a collection of Taylor family photos.

## THE PUN ALSO RISES

Inspired by the series of geological dips and bends with steep, rocky walls that surround the city, "Ithaca is Gorges" has been embraced as both unofficial slogan and defining identity of the city, and is famously printed on t-shirts and bumper stickers.  The "grammatically incorrect" slogan was the brainstorm of Howard Cogan who ran a local advertising agency and taught advertising and public relations at Ithaca College, prompted by the Chamber of Commerce who asked Cogan for an idea to help increase tourism in the area.  The ubiquitous t-shirt, usually green with white letters with a waterfall replacing the letter "I," has become an indie icon and has been seen literally all over the globe.

*Factoid*:  The logo has been the template for such spinoffs as "Ithaca is Boring," "Ithaca is Gangsta," and "Ithaca is Cold."

## THE LAKE MONSTER MYSTERY

Native Americans believed Seneca Lake to be a bottomless lake, with a monster that lived in its depths.  In his account published in the July 15, 1899 edition of *The Geneva Gazette*, geologist George R. Elwood describes the mysterious creature he observed in the lake: "About twenty-five feet long, with a tail which tapers until within about five feet of the end, where it broadens out to look much like a whale.  Its head is approximately four feet long and triangular in shape. Its mouth is very long and was armed with two rows of triangular white teeth as sharp as those of a shark, but in shape more like those of a sperm whale.  Its body is covered with a horny substance which is as much like the carapace of a terrapin which is brown in color and of a greenish tinge. Its eyes are round like those of a fish."

*Factoid*:  At 38 miles long and more than 400 feet deep, the bottom of Cayuga Lake dips below sea level.  And some say there's no telling what lives in the murky darkness.  In 1818, a canal was opened between Cayuga and Seneca Lakes, a fact that may connect Elwood's sighting to "Old Greeny," the eel-like creature found of Cayuga Lake lore.  Sightings of the strange creature were reported in *The Ithaca Journal* over the years from 1887 to 1979.

## ALL SPRUCED UP

A student at Cornell University and member of Delta Kappa Epsilon fraternity, Clifton Beckwith Brown left his studies at the outbreak of the Spanish American War to serve in Company M of the 71st New York Regiment alongside Colonel Teddy Roosevelt's Rough Riders.  Brown died in combat at the Battle of San Juan Hill on July 1, 1898, becoming the first Cornellian casualty of the war.  Returning a war hero, Roosevelt was elected Governor of New York, and on June 20, 1899, Governor Roosevelt, who was a member of Delta Kappa Epsilon fraternity at Harvard, visited the Cornell campus to plant two spruce trees at the castle-like DKE lodge in memory of his fallen comrade.

*Factoid*:  The mighty Norway spruce trees stand today at 13 South Avenue in Ithaca as a tribute to Brown's sacrifice.  They are listed on the New York State Register of Historic Trees.

## DUELING HALLS OF FAME

Susan B. Anthony was probably the most influential American woman of the 19th century.  Born in Massachusetts on February 15, 1820, she inherited the liberal reform tradition of her Quaker family. In 1851, she met Elizabeth Cady Stanton, who had launched the movement for women's rights on a national level in Seneca Falls. From that moment on, the two combined their strengths to spearhead the suffrage movement, raising public awareness and lobbying the government to grant voting rights to women. (Matilda Goslyn Gage, mother-in-law of L. Frank Baum, author the *The Wizard of Oz*, often visited Elizabeth Cady Stanton in Seneca Falls, as both were active in the woman's rights movement). After the National Women's Hall of Fame was opened on Fall Street in Seneca Falls, the men who drink at Red's Place across the street decided things had gone far enough and posted a response in the window: "Men's Hall of Fame."

*Factoid*: The Howland Stone Store was opened in 1837 in the hamlet of Sherwood, just north of King Ferry, by Slocum Howland, a Quaker, an abolitionist, prohibitionist and suffragist. The Howland Stone Store now operates as a museum, and its prized possession is an historical slice of cake from Susan B. Anthony's birthday celebration.

## COMFORT ZONE

The prominent point at Sheldrake-on-Cayuga is not natural topography, but rather a construction of gravelly loam "fill" carted in by horses during the early nineteenth century, to create bedding for a hamlet of summer cottages and gracious lakefront estates. Sheldrake provided the summer home of screenwriter, playwright, and television producer Rod Serling, creator of *The Twilight Zone*. Serling named his production company Cayuga Productions, and he wrote many of the series' 252 scripts in his lakeside cottage. His final resting place can be found in section G of Lake View Cemetery, County Road 150, in nearby Interlaken.

*Factoid*: The Point's agricultural legacy includes a 160-acre orchard and dairy farm, operated from 1850 until the mid-1980s, now the site of Sheldrake Point Vineyard. Although the average depth of the lake is 179 feet, just off the beach at Sheldrake, it plunges to 435 feet. Since deep water heats and cools more slowly, it delays both onset of the first frost in fall, lengthening the growing season of grapes to 170 days, more than two weeks longer than many other areas in the Finger Lakes.

## THE MAN WHO GAVE AWAY DIMES

The second of six children, John Davison Rockefeller was born in the Tioga County village of Richford on July 8, 1839. When he was a boy, his family moved to Moravia, and in 1851, to Owego, where he attended Owego Academy. As the founder of Standard Oil, he gradually gained almost complete control of oil refining and marketing in the United States. With significant interests in banking, shipping, mining, railroads, and other industries, his net worth continued to grow, and in personal wealth acquired, Rockefeller became the richest man in the world. He was a straight-laced, deeply devout Baptist. He believed that for every dime he gave away he would receive a dollar, and he became famous for passing out shiny new dimes to folks he passed on the street. Rockefeller gave out some $35,000 worth of dimes during his lifetime.

*Factoid*: Among his philanthropic contributions, Rockefeller donated $12,000 to build Ithaca's First Baptist Church at 309 North Cayuga Street. He later donated $250,000 to Cornell for Rockefeller Hall, the largest and best-equipped physics laboratory in America. (It is said he was so disappointed with the appearance of the red brick building, he vowed to never donate another cent to Cornell).

## LADY OF THE LAKES

On September 26, 2015, fifty-two-year-old Bridgette Hobart Janeczko of Binghamton, emerged from the southern end of Owasco Lake, having completed her quest to swim the length of nine of eleven Finger Lakes, the first documented person to do so. She started by swimming Canandaigua Lake. After that she tackled Keuka, Skaneateles, Cayuga, Seneca, Honeoye, Conesus, Otisco, and Owasco.

*Factoid*: Janeczko had originally planned to swim all eleven Finger Lakes, but was notified by the DEC that Hemlock and Canadice Lakes are both water sources for the city of Rochester and that no swimming was allowed.

## BENJAMIN FRANKLIN'S HARMONICA

In 1762, Benjamin Franklin invented a glass harmonica, using tuned glass bowls arranged in a long, horizontal tube configuration. Musicians played the instrument by wetting their fingers and running it along the bowls. Artists such as Wolfgang Amadeus Mozart and Ludwig van Beethoven were intrigued by the instrument, and composed pieces featuring Franklin's invention. In the early twentieth century, musician and collector Virginia Sturm rescued the strange instrument from obscurity, performing music during recitals and lectures. Her glass harmonica is now a part of the Corning Museum of Glass's collection.

*Factoid*: Corning Museum of Glass in the Steuben County city of Corning is home to the world's largest collection of glass, containing nearly 50,000 objects representing 3,500 years of glass history. It's one of the biggest and oldest museums in America and the third most popular tourist attraction in New York State, drawing 325,000 visitors annually.

## FREAK OF NATURE

The flowing waters of Glen Creek sculptured an incredibly scenic gorge with high cliffs, carved potholes, sparkling pools, and dramatic waterfalls. This extraordinary freak of nature was certainly known to the native Seneca Indians, but its name comes from Dr. Samuel Watkins and his brother John who acquired land in the area in the 1850s (the town was named "Watkins" in 1854 after Samuel's death). Watkins Glen was first realized as a tourist attraction by newspaperman and promoter Morvalden Ellis, who made sections of the gorge accessible by stairways and improved paths. Officially opened to the public on July 4, 1863, the 2-mile gorge trail includes 832 steps and gains 500 feet of elevation, passing over and under 19 waterfalls. In 1906, the State of New York acquired the Glen and opened it as a state park, now under the control of the New York State Parks Department.

*Factoid*: The second waterfall along the trail was named Minnehaha Falls by Ellis, inspired by the water-carved, heart-shaped pool at the base he advertised as a tribute to the love between Hiawatha and Minnehaha, as described in Longfellow's poem "Song of Hiawatha."

## THE GOOD, THE BAD, AND THE UGLY

Lithuania-born sculptor Jacques Lipchitz spent much of his early career in Paris, working alongside Pablo Picasso and Georges Braque as a leader of the Cubist movement. In 1982, Cornell University acquired "Song of the Vowels" a sculpture Lipchitz created in 1931. Among seven copies, Cornell's is the fifth. Other copies can be found at Princeton, UCLA, Stanford, and Nelson Rockefeller's Kykuit Gardens. Upon installation at Cornell, students were appalled at its peculiar shapes and bewildered by its reference to the harp. They called it "Song of the Bowels."

*Factoid*: In January 1983, Jason Seley, sculptor and dean of the Cornell University College of Architecture, gave Cornell '"Herakles in Ithaka I." His 11-foot, gently humorous interpretation of the Farnese Hercules used chromium-plated steel and automobile bumpers artfully contrived so that viewers are sometimes unaware that they are looking at car parts.

# HOOP DREAMS

After picking, fresh fruit was traditionally packed into baskets, then hauled to a dock or depot from which it shipped. The peach basket was uniquely designed with a flared top so fruit on the bottom was less likely to be squashed in shipment, and safely delivered to market. The invention of machinery that manufactured baskets using staples and a production line was important to this process, and the Yates Lumber Company in Penn Yan was one of the first basket manufacturers to use the machine. Edson Potter, president of the company, traveled to fruit markets around the Northeast, carrying his company's sample peach baskets to show to prospective buyers. It was at a market in New Haven, Connecticut that James Naismith, a physical education teacher visiting from Springfield, Massachusetts, ordered a dozen of Potter's baskets. After nailing a basket up at each end of his gym, the first game of basketball was played with a soccer ball and two peach baskets used as goals.

*Factoid*: The original basketball goals retained the basket bottoms for a time, so it was necessary, after each score, for an official to poke the ball back out for resumption of play. However, in the years which followed, the bottoms disappeared from the baskets and they evolved into the rims of steel, with netted sides.

# ROOSEVELT'S TREE ARMY

America's Great Depression began with a catastrophic collapse of stock -market prices on the New York Stock Exchange in October 1929. With nearly one-third of the country's work force unemployed, President Franklin Roosevelt created a public work relief program called the Civilian Conservation Corps. Under the guidance of the Departments of the Interior and Agriculture, C.C.C. employees fought forest fires, cleared and maintained access roads, re-seeded grazing lands and planted trees across the region by the tens of thousands. From 1933 to 1941, a C.C.C. camp was established near the Old Mill at Upper Treman Park in Enfield. More than 100 young men wore uniforms, and lived under quasi-military discipline, first in tents and later in wooden barracks complete with mess and recreation halls, shower and infirmary buildings. The men of the camp improved many of the region's trails, building stone bridges and stairways throughout public parks.

*Factoid*: Initials and names of some of these men inscribed in the cliff walls may be found in various places along the trails, often with the letters "C.C.C."

## BANANA BELT

Most of the vineyards in the Finger Lakes are located close to the lakes. Essentially, the lakes act as a moderating influence for surrounding temperatures, since water changes temperature at a much slower rate than air, maintaining temperature (whether warm or cool) for a longer period of time. Because lakes retain heat, they warm surrounding land, preventing roots from freezing during cold winters and protecting vines against sudden spring frosts and freezes. The lake effect is also helpful at the end of the growing season, allowing temperatures to remain warm enough for grapes to ripen on the vine into autumn.

*Factoid*: The combined effects of moderated temperature and precipitation are responsible for unique viticultural subregions such as the southeastern shore of Seneca Lake, known locally as the "banana belt."

## WORLD'S SMALLEST CHURCH

The structure at the intersection of Robbins Road and Harrisburg Hollow Road (between Bath and Hammondsport) is not a tiny church at all, but rather an effort to preserve the last remnants of the Methodist

Episcopal Church that once stood near the corner. The historic church had been built in 1891, but suffered a fire and most of the structure was ruined. This roadside wonder is the remaining steeple that survived the fire, and has been left in place to remember the church.

*Factoid*: The actual smallest church is Cross Island Chapel which still sits in the center of a pond on the northern edge of Oneida in Madison County. A small billboard near the road explains: "Built in 1989. Floor area 51" x 81" (28.68 square feet) Seats 2 people. Non-denominational."

## ASSASSINATION VACATION

A young man arrived in Canandaigua on April 16, 1865. He signed the register at the Webster House as "John Harrison," but his real name was John Harrison Surratt Jr. His mother, Mary, owned the boarding house in Washington, D.C. where John Wilkes Booth plotted Lincoln's assassination. Surratt left Canandaigua at noon on Monday, April 17, and headed for Canada, where a Catholic priest provided refuge. While there, he learned that his mother had been arrested, tried and hanged for conspiracy. With the help of former rebels, he left Canada under an assumed name, arrived in England and made his way to Rome. But he was recognized, arrested and jailed. Next he escaped to Egypt, where he was apprehended, returned to the United States, and made to stand trial in 1867. His defense – that he was nowhere near Washington on the night of the assassination – included testimony by the people he saw in Canandaigua and by his signature in the hotel register. After a two-month trial, the jury could not agree. He was ultimately freed.

*Factoid*: It was later learned that Surratt met Booth in 1864 and agreed to help him kidnap Lincoln, transport the president to the Confederate capital at Richmond and exchange him for thousands of rebel prisoners of war. On March 17, 1865, Surratt, Booth and their co-conspirators waited to ambush Lincoln's carriage as it traveled to the Soldiers' Home outside of Washington.  But Lincoln changed his mind and stayed in the city that day. The plot was foiled.

## TWO BUCKEROO

The Seneca Lodge, built by native son Don Brubaker in 1947, sits above Old Corning Hill in Watkins Glen near the upper entrance to the State Park.  The legendary lodge has been a post-race gathering place since the 1948 Grand Prix, the first post-WWII road race in America.  The walls of the bar are loaded with memorabilia, including the winner's laurel wreathes presented to James Hunt, Jackie Stewart, Emerson Fittipaldi and other legends following Formula One victories, which ran at the Glen from 1961 through 1980, as well as hundreds of arrows shot into the wall by ace archers who frequent the lodge for archery championships.

*Factoid*:  In longstanding tradition, the bartender at Seneca Lodge hands your change back in $2 bills.  There's even a special slot in the register for them — the drawer is organized to hold $1, $2, $5, $10, $20.

## BRAIN DEPOSITORY

The Wilder Brain Collection is a 120-year acquisition of human brains reminiscent of a gag in Mel Brooks' *Young Frankenstein*, maintained by the Cornell Department of Psychology on the second floor of Uris Hall on the university campus.  The collection was created by professor of anatomy, Burt Green Wilder, who served as a surgeon with the 55th Massachusetts Regiment during the American Civil War.  Wilder founded the Cornell Brain Society in 1889 to procure the brains of "educated and orderly persons," believing that much could be learned about psychology from studying the anatomy of the brain.  Among 600 specimens is the brain of Edward H. Rulloff, a career criminal known as "The Genius Killer." Rulloff's brain is said to be the second largest brain on record.

*Factoid*: The memory of Rulloff lives on in Ithaca. A bar at 411 College Avenue, just off the Cornell campus, bears his name.

## BIGFOOT

During the summer of 1869, a wild man was spotted by at least one hundred residents in the vicinity of Woodhill and Troupsville, just west of Corning. He made shrieking sounds as he raced through the countryside. According to local newspapers, an eyewitness said he moved "with a springing, jerking hitch in his gait that gave him more the appearance of a wild animal than a human being." One man got a close-up view: "The long, matted hair; the thick, black, uncombed beard; the wild, glaring, bloodshot eyeballs, which seemed bursting from their sockets; the swage, haggard, unearthly countenance; the wild, beastly appearance of this thing, whether man or animal, has haunted me"

*Factoid*: Native Americans in the region believe Bigfoot is a spirit creature and that is why he will never be captured.

## CARTOON CHARACTER

Born in Basel, Switzerland on May 26, 1862, Eugene Zimmerman immigrated to the United States with his family in 1868. He became an apprentice sign painter, while nurturing a desire to become a professional cartoonist. In May 1883, with the help of Joseph Keppler, director of *Puck Magazine*, he was hired at the humor magazine, dropping the last portion of his signature to become "Zim." He married Mabel Alice Beard of Horseheads and made the Chemung County town his home. Becoming one of America's best-known cartoonists, Zimmerman published more than 40,000 sketches during his lifetime.

*Factoid*: In Horseheads, Zim designed the town's Teal Park Band-stand. Whimsical carvings on the gazebo reflect his cartoon fantasies, including giant crickets playing fiddles.

## DANGEROUS LOCATION

In August of 1935, Bette Davis arrived in Ithaca with her co-star Franchot Tone to shoot exteriors for the Warner Bros. film, *Dangerous*. Tone was an alum of Cornell University, Class of '27, and the trip provided him the opportunity to visit his alma mater. The Ithaca location was a stand-in for a "gentleman's farm" in Connecticut, and the pivotal scene took place on the bridge over Fall Creek gorge.

*Factoid*: Davis won the Academy Award for Best Actress for her performance in the film, but always felt it was a consolation prize for not having been nominated for *Of Human Bondage* the previous year.

## WHAT TO SEE AT THE LOUVRE

Known as "Tumbling Waters" to the Native Americans, Shequaga Falls is a frothy cascade that pours down the cliff-side on the western edge of the Schuyler County village Montour Falls. It appears to start from the arch bridge above and fans out, tumbling at various degrees over gray limestone and reaching the shallow plunge pool below. The creek then turns 90-degrees to the north and continues on its way to Seneca Lake.

*Factoid*: Louis Philippe, king of France from 1830 to 1848, spent more than three years in American exile, from 1796 to 1800. On his visit to the Finger Lakes region, he made a painting of Shequaga Falls. That painting is on display at the Louvre Museum in France.

## LAST BEST HOPE

John Nicholas Rose, the son of Robert and Jane Rose, journeyed to the Finger Lakes region from the family plantation in Stafford County,

Virginia. He purchased 1,000 acres of land at Bluff Point and completed construction of the home he called "Esperanza" (derived from the Latin word for "hope") in 1838. The largest house on Keuka Lake at the time, its rectangular form and classical details were firmly rooted in Greek Revival tradition, and the two-story ionic columns at its entrance were built around giant tree trunks encased in brick and stucco. In this bucolic setting, John Rose raised English-bred Saxon sheep and profited handsomely from selling high-quality wool. Over the years, Esperanza has served as head-quarters for a vineyard operation, a 1000-acre farm, home to several distinguished families, a link in the Underground Railroad, the county poorhouse, a commercial winery, and although transformed into a luxury resort and conference center in 2003, Esperanza Mansion was foreclosed on by Genesee Regional Bank in 2018.

*Factoid*: Esperanza is said to be the home of the "Lady in White," a ghostly apparition who roams the grounds of the estate, although it is unclear who she is or why she is there.

## CORNELL SPELLED BACKWARDS

In 1867, Ezra Cornell began construction of a sprawling mansion he called "Llenroc" (the backwards spelling of his name) on a knoll overlook-ing Ithaca and Cayuga Lake. He hired an Albany firm, Nichols and Brown, to design a plan which borrowed heavily from both Gothic and High Victorian styles. Irish, Scottish, and Italian immigrants, as well as Native Americans, were employed as laborers. German artisans were commis-sioned to carve elaborate designs into the native bluestone, hauled from a quarry just west of White Hall on the Arts Quad, while English artisans were hired to carve the woodwork. Eight complete marble fireplaces were imported from Europe and placed throughout the house. The phrase "True and Firm" was carved over the entryway at the suggestion of university president Andrew Dickson White.

*Factoid*: Sadly, Ezra did not get to live in his dream house. He died in 1874, a year before the project was completed. Ownership of Llenroc at 100 Cornell Avenue remained in the Cornell family until 1911, when the house was purchased by the Delta Phi fraternity.

## BASED ON A TRUE STORY

In 1905, Chester Ellsworth Gillette took a position at his uncle's skirt factory in Cortland. At the factory, Gillette met Grace Brown, another employee, and the two began a sexual relationship. In spring 1906, Brown revealed that she was pregnant and pressured Gillette to marry her, often writing him pleading letters. The couple made arrangements for a summer trip to Big Moose Lake in Herkimer County, and on July 11, Gillette took Brown out on the lake in a rowboat where he clubbed her with his tennis racquet and left her to drown. Gillette was charged with her murder and the trial took place in Herkimer County. Gillette was found guilty, and on March 30, 1908, he was executed by electric chair at Auburn Prison.

*Factoid*: The story was basis for the fictional character Clyde Griffiths in Theodore Dreiser's 1925 novel *An American Tragedy*, the basis of the 1951 film *A Place in the Sun* with Montgomery Clift and Shelly Winters as the tragic couple.

## UNDER AND OVER THE BRIDGE

In the early days of roadways, bridges were typically constructed from wood, which was plentiful, inexpensive and a fitting structural material. Exposed wooden bridges would eventually deteriorate after exposure to the elements, so to enable a more durable and long-lasting structure, bridges were built with a cover, in most cases including both a roof and sides. In the town of Newfield, a few miles south of Ithaca, stands the oldest surviving covered bridge still open to daily vehicular traffic. It crosses the west branch of the Cayuga Creek in a single span of 115 feet. When the bridge was first built in 1853, it had solid siding, but later diamond-shaped windows were cut to let light in.

*Factoid*: Newfield is one of the only communities in the nation to maintain both a covered bridge developed in the Agricultural Era and a King Iron Bowstring Bridge constructed during the Industrial Revolution. At 222 Main Street, the King Bowstring Arch Bridge is one of the earliest prefabricated bridges and one of only five Zenas King Bridges left in New York State.

## THE ART OF DUNKING

"Dunking" donuts became popular when Clark Gable taught Claudette Colbert how to dunk in Frank Capra's 1934 film, *It Happened One Night*. Since 1929, Wager's Cider Mill at 256 East Main Street, just outside the village of Penn Yan, has been squeezing local apples into cider and frying the region's best donuts, made fresh daily.

*Factoid*: Wager's cider press was brought from Geneva, where it was built in 1883.

## THE DOCTOR IS A LADY

In October 1847, a young woman by the name of Elizabeth Blackwell applied for acceptance to Hobart College in Geneva, then called Geneva Medical College. The dean and faculty, usually responsible for evaluating an applicant, were not able to make a decision due to the special nature of Blackwell's case. They put the issue up to a vote by the 150 male students of the class with the stipulation that if one student objected, Blackwell would be turned away. The young men voted unanimously to accept her. In the summer between her two terms at Geneva, she worked at Blockley Almshouse (later known as Philadelphia General Hospital), although some young resident physicians still would walk out and refuse to assist her in diagnosing and treating her patients. During her time there, Blackwell primarily cared for those afflicted with typhus, and her graduating thesis was on the topic of typhus. On January 23, 1849, Elizabeth Blackwell became the first woman to achieve a medical degree in the United States.

*Factoid*: The local press reported her graduation favorably, and when the dean, Dr. Charles Lee, conferred her degree, he stood up and bowed to her.

## WORLD'S BEST HOT DOG STAND

The idea of getting a decent "wiener" while on the hoof along the Seneca Lake wine trail is the brainstorm of Master Sommelier Christopher Bates. But the FLX Wienery at 5090 Route 14 in Dundee is not your average hot dog shack. Step up to the counter for Zweigle's Red Dogs or White Hots, served single or double with creative topping combos and irresistible sides. And here's where it gets interesting. You can wash down your dog with a bottle from the "Secret Wine Fridge," an astonishing hodgepodge of well-priced gems from Mr. Bates' personal collection.

*Factoid*: If you've already picked up a bottle of local wine at one of the nearby tasting rooms, bring it in. There's no corkage fee.

## MARK TWAIN'S FATHER-IN-LAW

Jervis Langdon was born on January 9, 1809 in the Oneida County village of Vernon. When he turned sixteen, he went to work in a country store in Vernon, then at a store in Ithaca, both owned by a Mr. Stevens. His boss found the boy dependable and hardworking, and sent him to open a branch in the neighboring village of Enfield. Langdon help organize the Enfield Presbyterian Church in 1832, the year he married Olivia Lewis. The couple moved to Elmira where he worked in the lumber business, then in the coal trade.  His operations eventually included mines in Pennsylvania and Nova Scotia, and a huge rail and shipping network supplying coal to western New York State and Chicago.  Jervis and Olivia Langdon had three children: Susan, Charles, and Olivia ("Livy"), who married Samuel Langhorne Clemens in 1870.

*Factoid*: An ardent abolitionist, Jervis Langdon served as a "stationmaster" on the Underground Railroad in Elmira and helped over 800 individuals find their way to freedom.  He counted Frederick Douglass, whom he helped to escape from slavery, among his friends.

## RUN AWAY AND JOIN THE CIRCUS

A space that once housed the printing presses of *The Ithaca Journal* is now home to a circus school, featuring features training in various circus skills such as acrobatics, contortion, juggling, unicycling, trapeze technique, and clowning.  Circus Culture at 116 West Green Street in Ithaca is the brainstorm of Amy Cohen, who trained with performers from the Big Apple Circus.

*Factoid*: According to research, circus skills allow students to increase their concentration, coordination, retention and reaction times.  In addition it enhances cross curricular learning, spatial awareness and peripheral vision as well as timing, rhythm, focus and motor skills.

## THE SANDS OF WINE

Marvin Sands established the Canandaigua Wine Company in 1945, making fruit wine in bulk in a converted sauerkraut factory.  In 1954, he launched a proprietary brand of wine called Richard's Wild Irish Rose, concocted from generic local grapes and named after his son Richard.  Sands skipped crucial, time-consuming steps in production, but spiked the product with brandy.  The pink liquid that ended up in the bottles had an appalling bouquet, but it flew off the shelves, giving the small winery its introduction to the big leagues of wine distribution on the national scene. By 1980, annual sales topped $50 million, and in 2000, the company changed its name to Constellation Brands to reflect its range of beverage products and brands.  In 2004, Constellation snapped up the iconic but struggling Robert Mondavi Corporation of Oakville, California for more than a billion dollars in cash.

*Factoid*:  Constellation Brands has become the world's biggest wine conglomerate, generating over $7 billion in annual revenue.

## FLOOD OF MEMORIES

Hurricane Agnes first came ashore on the Florida Panhandle on June 19, 1972 and moved north through Georgia and the Carolinas.  The hurricane then went out to sea, recharged its energy, and returned to hit the Finger Lakes region on June 22.  There was flooding along Oneida and Skaneateles lakes, and waters rushed through downtown Auburn.  But Elmira and Corning took the hardest hit.  Three days of torrential rain washed out the business districts of both cities, chasing tens of thousands from their homes.  Water overcame 23-foot dikes in raging currents that tore houses from foundations, ripped up highways, and helped fuel the oncoming economic recession of the 1970s.  Overall, Agnes caused 128 fatalities and nearly $3 billion in damage.  Due to the devastation caused by Agnes, the name "Agnes" was retired from use in naming storms in 1973.

*Factoid*:  In July 7 and 8, 1935, a slow-moving low pressure system stalled along a cold front in central New York, merged with a system which had moved up the coast, and then intensified.  Known nationally as the "Finger Lakes Flood," the historic deluge dropped nearly a foot of rain within 48 hours in the region.  In the aftermath of the 1935 event, the final death toll would skyrocket to over 50 region-wide.

# CLIFFHANGERS

When brothers Theo and Leo Wharton arrived in Ithaca to film a Cornell football game for the Essanay Film Company, they found the local topography perfect for thrilling stunts in serials and features. In April of 1914, they built a movie studio, including indoor and outdoor stages, on the southernmost shore of Cayuga Lake in Ithaca (now the site of Stewart Park), where they produced more than 100 films of the silent era. The term "cliffhanger" comes from the weekly episodes in which a heroine would end up hanging over a cliff as a villain waited for her to plummet to her death. Theater audiences would need to return the following week to find out how the heroine escaped. The most popular Wharton serials were *The Exploits of Elaine*, starring Pearl White, and *Patria*, starring Irene Castle, both female protagonists, variously chased, rescued and wooed. Unfortunately for Ithaca, the moviemaking industry left town and headed for Hollywood in 1920.

*Factoid*: Other early movie stars who worked in Ithaca include Lionel Barrymore, Francis X. Bushman, Beverly Bayne, Warner Oland (later gaining fame as "Charlie Chan") and Oliver Hardy (before teaming with Stan Laurel).

# GOLDILOCKS SLEPT HERE

Originally known as Brink's Tavern, the Three Bear Inn in the Cortland County town of Marathon takes its name, not from the fairy tale, but from three bearskins that once hung on the front porch. There is still much to see in the way of the inn's 200-year history. In addition to the three stuffed bears in the foyer, old photographs grace the walls, as well as an antique phone, stove, furniture and an old bear trap.

*Factoid*: Since Marathon happens to be 26.2 miles from Ithaca, an annual long-distance endurance race connected the two towns for 25 consecutive years, inspired by the legend of Pheidippides, a Greek soldier and runner who was sent from Marathon to Athens to announce that the Persians had been defeated in the Battle of Marathon.

## VANISHED VIKING VILLAGE

The bluff above Y-shaped Keuka Lake is the site of the most mysterious set of ancient structures ever reported in the Finger Lakes region. These prehistoric structures were built even before the period of Iroquois habitation around the lake. Who built them is still not known for certain, despite years of research. The ruins are comprised of well-arranged stone floors and slab hedgerows. Stones dividing the sections are well cut, resembling small slabs, and are placed in the ground in an elaborate, extensive, grid-pattern. There are similar in appearance to sites in Europe, most like a Norse settlement on the Brough of Birsay, a tidal island in the Orkney Islands, near Skara Brae, in Scotland.

*Factoid*: The Viking exploration of North America began in the late 10th century AD, and the Bluff Point Stoneworks seem to suggest a village of Nordic origin. Norse records indicate that in 1347 there were several expeditions to a new land in the West.

## THE PRUSSIAN WHO HELPED SAVE AMERICA

Steuben County was named after Baron Friedrich Wilhelm Von Steuben, the Prussian military officer who became a Revolutionary War hero, serving under General Washington at Valley Forge. The Baron, who is credited with teaching volunteers the essentials of military drills, tactics, and disciplines, swore and yelled his recruits in German and French, and when that was no longer successful, he recruited Captain Benjamin Walker, his French-speaking aid to curse at them in English. He became Washington's chief of staff during the final years of the war. The Baron, by the way, never lived in his eponymous county.  Granted a $2,500 yearly pension after the war, he settled in Oneida County on a small estate near Rome.

*Factoid*:  Steuben Glass Works was an art glass manufacturer, founded in the summer of 1903 by Frederick Carder and Thomas G. Hawkes in Corning in Steuben County from which the company name was derived. In 1918, Steuben was acquired by Corning Glass Works.

## NAME GAME

A distinguished business and political figure in the city of Geneva, Castner Emmet Rapalee served as mayor of that city for one term.  In its century-plus history, Geneva has elected over thirty persons as its head, and of those individuals, the name of Castner Emmet Rapalee is the oddest. Rapalee was born in the town of Bath on December 29, 1884.  His term as mayor lasted from 1948 to1950.

*Factoid*:  Shotwell Powell, a prominent 19th century resident of the Ontario County town of Naples was elected to two terms in the New York State Assembly in 1859 and 1860.

## THE KIDS ARE ALRIGHT

William Reuben George was a native of West Dryden, near Freeville, who as a businessman in New York City became interested in the problem of youth gangs, and he began to organize members into more productive groups who helped, rather than hindered the police.  He wanted to give neglected or wayward youths some of the summer fresh air and fun he had experienced as a child on the family farm, and in the summer of 1890, he brought 22 children to Freeville with funds received from *The New York Tribune*, sponsors of The Fresh Air Fund charity.  Over the early years, he slowly developed his idea of a Junior Republic with laws made by young "citizens" and an economic system controlled by youngsters.  Today, a broad range of programs engage at-risk youths, treating mental, physical, and emotional needs while teaching responsibility, citizenship, and the skills that will help them grow into productive members of society.

*Factoid*: Annually, more than 3,000 youths are served through community-based services at Junior Republic residential campuses in multiple states and counties.

## VIOLIN LESSONS

Leaving his Danby home as a young man for violin studies abroad, William Grant Egbert confided his desire to establish a conservatory in nearby Ithaca so that others wouldn't need to travel so far from home to study music. When he returned from lessons in Berlin, Germany, he assembled eight faculty members and two lecturers. On September 19, 1892, with an enrollment of 125 students, the Ithaca Conservatory of Music began lessons in four rented rooms in a house on East Seneca Street. Instruction was given in violin (taught by Egbert), voice (by Gertrude Walker Egbert), keyboard and string instruments, history, biography, and modern fencing. By 1897, studies in elocution, dance, physical education, speech correction, radio, business, and the liberal arts were added to the curriculum. In 1910, the school had secured permanent quarters with the purchase of Judge Douglass Boardman's handsome Italianate townhouse at 120 East Buffalo Street, adjoining DeWitt Park.

*Factoid*: In 1931, Egbert's conservatory became Ithaca College, offering dozens of majors within the schools of Business, Communications, Health Sciences and Human Performance, Humanities and Sciences, and of course, Music.

## WATER CURE

The year was 1871. The place was Slaterville, a village eight miles southeast of Ithaca named in honor of early settler Levi Slater. Dr. William Gallagher discovered that "magnetic waters" from local springs and wells had "curative," "health-giving," even "magical" properties. In 1893, Slaterville spring water won an award at the Columbian Exposition in Chicago for its clarity and excellence. Three hotels were built nearby the village for the "rest and water cure" trade, where guests soaked in tubs filled with the spring water as a purported cure for all sorts of ills. Business declined by 1920 when the water cure fad faded.

*Factoid*: The "ambering" effect of the spring water was first noticed in 1871 by a Slaterville Springs resident named Mrs. Middaugh, who sold colored glass to hotel guests. In 1967, Clarence Stephens began using local spring water to create "Art Glass," the process of leaving glassware in the water for several weeks and tinting them to the color of iced tea. The Stephens operation ended in the 1990s, but water "ambering" became something of a cottage industry in the hamlet, with other local residents continuing the process.

## GROUND CONTROL TO COMMANDER COLLINS

Born in Elmira on November 19, 1956, a graduate of Elmira Free Academy and alumnus of Syracuse University, Eileen Marie Collins became the Air Force's first female flight instructor in 1979, and for the next 11 years taught both flying and math. Selected as an astronaut in 1990, Collins became the first woman pilot of a U.S. space shuttle in February 1995, serving on the orbiter Discovery for a rendezvous and docking mission to the Russian space station Mir.

*Factoid*: With hundreds of hours in space to her credit, Collins became the first woman to command a shuttle mission in July 1999, taking Columbia into Earth orbit to deploy the Chandra X-ray Observatory.

# WHEN THE RAILROAD LEAVES TOWN

The Lehigh Valley Railroad ended passenger service to Ithaca when the last Black Diamond Express rolled out of town on May 11, 1959. The former Ithaca station sat empty until 1963 when it reopened as The Station restaurant. Patrons dined in the passenger waiting room, baggage claim, the ticket-office-turned-barroom, or aboard the rail coaches, which had been converted into dining cars, carpeted with surplus stock originally woven for the Pullman Coach Company. Time on the 18-foot Seth Thomas, four-faced railroad clock out front never changed, its hands set to the time when the last Black Diamond Express departed Ithaca.

*Factoid*: After the restaurant closed in 2005, the building was repurposed as the Ithaca branch of Elmira-based Chemung Canal Trust Company.

# CUCKOO'S NEST

During the mid-nineteenth century, the efforts of Dorothea Lynde Dix helped create dozens of new institutions for the mentally ill across the United States and Europe, intent on changing people's perceptions of these populations. The largest of the asylums built in response to her campaigning was the Willard Asylum for the Insane, located on the shore of Seneca Lake and County Road 132 near Ovid, named for Dr. Sylvester D. Willard, secretary of the state medical society in New York. In 1866, Mary Rote, a woman born with physical deformities, became Patient No.1, and within months, Willard was filled to its 250-bed capacity. In 1890, the facility was renamed the Willard State Hospital, housing more than 2,000 patients, and by the turn of the century, more than 3,000 patients. Many of the residents thought they were only going for a short stay, but ended up spending the rest of their lives there. They could be committed for various reasons, such as "feeblemindedness," having mental and physical handicaps, or being gay or lesbian.

*Factoid*: By the early 1990s, there was increasing stigma around insane asylums, and in 1995, Willard closed its doors for good. The closure of asylums has not been matched with necessary levels of community care and in some ways, the mentally ill are worse off than they were before. Many mentally ill have ended up homeless, or in the care of family members who often struggle to give them the care they need.

## LEGEND OF THE PAINTED ROCKS

Paintings on the sheer cliffs at the southern end of Seneca Lake appear to depict the Seneca tribe's escape from General John Sullivan's campaign to wipe out Indian settlements in the region. Many believe that the Indians made these pictographs in order to record the history of the event, as rock art historically played an important part in Native American story-telling. Older images, located near the bottom of the cliffs, may have been painted from canoes using organic materials. The pictographs are visible only from the water, so to view the Painted Rocks, you'll need a boat.

*Factoid*: It is known that the more visible and prominent paintings of the Indians, American flag, and teepee were added in 1929 during the Sullivan Sesquicentennial. There is an obvious mistake in these 1929 additions. Native tribes in the region lived in longhouses, not teepees.

## JOLLY TROLLEY

After Brooklyn and Binghamton, Ithaca was the third city in New York State to install an electric trolley system. In 1887, the first track was laid, extending from the Lehigh Valley railroad station to Ithaca Hotel. In 1892, threatened with competition for passengers, horse-drawn carriage operators hired a Cornell engineering professor to declare that trolleys could not possibly climb East Hill. But climb they did, powered by hydroelectricity from Six Mile Creek, Cascadilla and Fall Creeks. One of Ithaca's most heavily traveled trolley lines ran from downtown up State Street to the Cornell campus. On a 1900 campaign trip to Ithaca, New York Governor and vice presidential candidate Teddy Roosevelt was transported from the Cornell campus into downtown in a decorated trolley car, with lines of cheering students and women waving hankerchiefs from porches and lawns along the way. 1935 marked the end of the trolley era in Ithaca.

*Factoid*: In 1914, a trolley car provided the most famous single scene ever filmed in Ithaca with a plunge off the Stewart Avenue bridge over Fall Creek gorge during the Wharton brothers' filming of The Kiss of Blood.

## BRIGHT IDEA

The city of Corning was named after Albany financier, Erastus Corning, one of the founding fathers, and Corning Glass Works, now Corning Incorporated, was named after the city. In 1879, a 32-year-old inventor named Thomas Edison approached Corning Glass with his idea for the lightbulb. He needed just the right glass to encase the delicate filaments that comprised the lightbulb. By 1880, Edison had designated Corning as his sole supplier of the glass bulbs he needed to bring light to the world. Corning developed the automated production of lightbulbs and by 1926, turning out 15,000 bulbs an hour.

*Factoid*: Corningware and Pyrex, two of America's most beloved household brands, were famously invented in Corning. Fiber optic cable for long distance telecommunication and high-speed data connection was developed by Corning in the 1960s and 70s

## THE POSTMASTER WHO COULDN'T SPELL

For his services in the Revolutionary War, Abner Treman received 600 acres of land, now in part occupied by Trumansburg. The village was once known as Shin Hollow because, legend says, folks bumped their shins on tree stumps as they made their way home from the local tavern. The village was later re-named for the Treman family, but was misspelled "Trumansburg" by Col. Hermon Camp, the postmaster (perhaps after visiting the same tavern), and so it has remained.

*Factoid*: Between 1961 and 1970, Trumansburg was home to Robert Moog who built electronic music equipment including Theremins and his famous synthesizers in a downtown storefront.

## HELLO DALAI

Since 1959, natives of Tibet have scattered throughout the world, fleeing the Communist Chinese occupation of their country. Among the first Tibetan refugees to arrive in Ithaca in 1992 was a monk from Namgyal, the Dalai Lama's monastery in Dharamsala, India. With his inspiration and the help of American friends, a Victorian house on Aurora Street was transformed into a cultural and religious center for the Tibetan community, growing to become the North American seat of His Holiness the 14th Dalai Lama, personally blessed during his visit to Ithaca in 2007. In 2014, the house was sold and Namgyal moved up to South Hill, establishing a new retreat center and monastery and offering students an opportunity to study the Tibetan Buddhist tradition. Visiting faculty include prominent western scholars, clergy, and teachers from all traditions.

*Factoid*: It was the Buddhist monks in Ithaca who helped Kurt Cobain along the path to his next life. The lead singer of grunge band Nirvana had been attracted to the spiritual practices of Tibetan Buddhism, and soon after his death, his widow, Courtney Love, brought two handfuls of his ashes to the Ithaca monastery to be consecrated. The ashes were mixed with clay, and transformed into the symbolic image of Buddha's heart.

# TEMPLES OF WINEMAKING

The Finger Lakes wine region has as impressive an array of architectural standouts. Rising from the surrounding vineyards like a mirage, the distinctive design of Lamoreaux Landing Wine Cellars in Lodi suggests a cross between Greek Revival architecture, common throughout the Finger Lakes, and one of the region's field barns. Built on a sloping hillock, it is rectangular and spare, its facing in redwood with windows, almost floor to ceiling, offering views of 25 miles of Seneca Lake. The American Institute of Architects named it one of the most notable buildings erected in New York State during the twentieth century.

*Factoid*: The Heron Hill Winery in Hammondsport was designed by New York City architect Charles Warren in 1999, combining many elements of the region. The observation tower in the center of the building is reminiscent of farm silos that dot the area's country hills. The nod to Greek Revival mimics a style common to homes and farms, and the stone cobbles that adorn both the inside and outside of the building recall old cobblestone houses built after clearing stony fields and vineyards.

# GUERILLA MARKETING

Ten years after a purported "petrified man" was uncovered in the Onondaga County hamlet of Cardiff and exhibited by P.T. Barnum as the remains of an authentic giant, Ithaca attracted thousands of tourists as the fame of the "Taughannock Giant" became subject of newspaper articles and intense speculation about his origins. On July 4, 1879, a seven-foot, 800-pound stone man was unearthed near the shore of Cayuga Lake, on the property of John Thompson, owner of the Taughannock House Hotel. The specimen was described as "a human figure lying on its back, arms nearly straight and the legs crossed at the ankle, well-proportioned with the exception of the feet, which appear more like those of an ape." After perhaps one too many drinks at the hotel bar, one of the men who had buried the giant revealed the hoax, conceived by Thompson for the purpose of promoting his hotel.

*Factoid*: After analyzing a sample of the body, Cornell scientists mistakenly proclaimed that it was an authentic petrifaction of a human of an extinct, prehistoric race.

## THE MOVIE STAR WHO STAYED FOR DINNER

As one-half of a dance team with husband Vernon, Irene Castle ushered ballroom dancing into vogue and bobbed hair (the "Castle Clip") into popular style. While Vernon was in the service, Irene arrived in Ithaca to star in *Patria*, an early Wharton Brothers serial. After Vernon was killed in an aviation accident, Irene met Robert Elias Treman of the Ithaca Tremans, and the two were married in May of 1919. After a honeymoon in Lake Placid, the Treman family gifted the newlyweds a huge stone house on Cayuga Heights Road (now the Sigma Chi fraternity). The Tremans had a Gatsbyesque time in a house filled with furniture from Wanamaker's, a swimming pool (only one in Ithaca) filled with salt water from Atlantic City, and a cellar filled with the entire contents of a New York City liquor store, closed by Prohibition.

*Factoid*: Although a banker by profession, Robert turned producer and starred his new wife in four films, all financial failures. The storybook marriage ended in 1923 when Irene discovered that Robert had invested her money in the movies, and that it had all gone down the drain.

## SWAMP HERMIT

Foster Parker was born in the Cayuga County town of Montezuma in 1858 and lived alone in the marshes near the Cayuga-Seneca Canal, reachable only by a plank boardwalk elevated over the swampland. Known as the "Swamp Hermit of the Finger Lakes," he was considered one of the best authorities in America on migratory fowl, frequently visited by ornithologists from all over the country. He spent most days raising wood ducks in captivity to supply to zoos and parks in many states, and mounting rare birds, muskrats and foxes.

*Factoid*: The wood duck is one of the most stunning of all waterfowl. Males are iridescent chestnut and green, with ornate patterns on nearly every feather, and the females have a distinctive profile and delicate white pattern around the eye.

## ANNIE GET YOUR GUN

The original Ithaca Gun Company factory was established in 1883 and once stood in the Fall Creek neighborhood of Ithaca, on a slope still known as Gun Hill, where the nearby waterfall supplied the main source of energy for the plant. Led by renowned arms designer William Henry Baker, the company advertised its shotguns and rifles as "the strongest, simplest, and best American guns manufactured." Ithaca field guns were lightweight, but rugged and simple, and famous for their fast lock-time. Prominent figures such as Teddy Roosevelt, John Philip Sousa, George Marshall, and Dwight Eisenhower were known to use Ithaca firearms. Ithaca guns gained legendary status in the hands of Annie Oakley, the sharpshooting superstar of Buffalo Bill's Wild West Show. Using a 12-gauge double-barreled field gun, Oakley could split a playing card edge-on and put five or six more holes in it before it touched the ground.

*Factoid*: Before the company's demise, Ithaca shotguns were used by Los Angeles and New York Police Departments, and sold to the Royal Thai Army in the early 1980s to arm farmers against Communist infiltrators.

# GRAND CANYON OF THE EAST

In 1859, industrialist William Pryor Letchworth began purchasing land in the Wyoming County town of Castile, and started construction of his Glen Iris Estate. In 1906 he bequeathed the 1,000-acre estate to New York State, which became the core of the newly created Letchworth State Park. The park prominently features three large waterfalls – the Upper, Middle, and Lower Falls – on the Genesee River, which flows within a deep gorge that winds through the park. The rock walls of the gorge, which rise up to 550 feet in places, prompted the area's reputation as the "Grand Canyon of the East." The historic, restored Glen Iris Inn, William Pryor Letchworth's former residence on the top of a cliff overlooking Middle Falls has been adapted for use as a hotel and offers in-season meals and overnight accommodations.

*Factoid*: The Gardeau Overlook looks down into the Genesee River Valley where Mary Jemison once lived. Mary was born mid-Atlantic in the autumn of 1743, on board the ship that was bringing her parents from Northern Ireland to America. During the French and Indian war, she was captured and adopted at age 15 by Native Americans. She eventually married a Seneca and raised seven children. Her story would later inspire the 1956 Western film, *The Searchers*, starring John Wayne.

# BRIDGE OVER TROUBLED WATERS

In 1800, a group of investors, associates of Vice President Aaron Burr, constructed a mile-long, 132-foot-wide wooden bridge that spanned the northern end of Cayuga Lake, allowing travelers to avoid the muck of the Montezuma wetlands. It was one of the early wonders of the Finger Lakes region and the longest bridge in the western world at the time. After ice caused the bridge to collapse in 1808, the ferry that had been replaced by the bridge returned to service until a shorter, more northern replacement bridge was built in 1813. By 1858, the idea for a third bridge across the lake was abandoned as competition from the Erie Canal and railroads proved to be too great.

*Factoid*: In both 1929 and 1930 the New York State legislature passed bills authorizing construction of a modern highway bridge over the ancient route of the original Cayuga Bridge. Opposition from the Finger Lakes Association prompted Governor Franklin Roosevelt to veto both bills.

## THE MAN WHO LOVED WINE

Paul Garrett, son of a Confederate surgeon, established his first winery, Garrett and Company, in North Carolina in 1900, producing the Virginia Dare wines, one of the nation's top selling brands. After the growing temperance movement in the South made North Carolina an unfriendly environment for a wine business, he expanded into the Finger Lakes, and by 1913, he owned vineyards and facilities in Canandaigua, Hammondsport and Penn Yan. During Prohibition, Garrett continued to make and distribute wine for sacramental purposes, one of the few legal uses permitted. He was the first winery executive to promote wine made from blending New York State and California grown grapes.

*Factoid*: The Garrett Chapel at Bluff Point in Penn Yan, also known as the "Little Chapel on the Mount," was erected in 1931 in memory of Garrett's son Charles, who died at age sixteen from then-untreatable "white plague" of tuberculosis. Offering scenic views of Keuka Lake, the chapel was added to the National Register of Historic Places in 2001.

## VIRGIN DETECTORS

On the East Hill Arts Quad, the site of Cornell's original academic buildings, a statue of founder Ezra Cornell stands between McGraw Hall and Morrill Hall, and a statue of the university's first president, Andrew

Dickson White, sits upon a chair in front of Goldwin Smith Hall. According to campus folklore, if a virgin crosses the quad as the clock tower strikes midnight, the statues will walk off their pedestals, meet in the center, and shake hands, congratulating each other on the chastity of the university. The legend is memorialized by a trail of footprints, first painted in 1927 by Hugh Troy, Ithaca's legendary practical joker, and repainted every year since.

*Factoid*: On the plaza of Ithaca College's Textor Hall stands "Disc," sculptor Jack Squier's 10-foot high, round metal interpretation of a fish, mounted over a small pool of water, and referred to by students as the "Textor Ball." It is said that when a virgin graduates from IC, the Textor Ball will roll off its pedestal and all the way down the hill. It has never moved.

## EIGHT IS ENOUGH

Octagonal houses were popularized in the United States in the mid-19th century by Orson Squire Fowler of Cohocton in Steuben County who touted the advantages of octagonal homes over rectangular and square structures in his widely publicized book, *The Octagon House: A Home For All, or A New, Cheap, Convenient, and Superior Mode of Building*. Today, by most estimates, less than 500 octagon buildings remain standing, a good many of them still dotting the Finger Lakes countryside. The VanBurkirk-Raines House on Gorham Street in Canandaigua was inhabited from 1872 to 1912 by Senator John Raines, built just before the Civil War. The Eight-Square Schoolhouse on Upper Hanshaw Road (1/4 mile east of the Tompkins County Regional Airport) is the earliest school still existing in Tompkins County, and the only surviving brick octagonal schoolhouse in New York State. The most historic 8-sided structure in the region sits on the campus of Elmira College. "It is the loveliest study you ever saw," Mark Twain wrote to a friend about the octagonal hilltop pavilion his in-laws provided him in 1874.

*Factoid*: In 1976, Bill Wagner broke ground on what would become the iconic octagon building that houses Wagner Winery in Lodi, specially designed with the cellars underground taking advantage of nature's cooling system.

## POOR MAN'S PIZZA

Generations of Cornell University students have satisfied late-night food cravings at two legendary food trucks, Louie's Lunch and the Hot Truck. Greek immigrant Louis "Louie" Zounakos started with a pushcart in 1918, eventually replaced with a Ford truck he parked across the street from Risley Hall, selling mostly cold subs and sandwiches. In the late 1940s, Louie bought a new truck, painted in Cornell colors of red and white, equipped with stainless steel counters and electrical facilities, custom-made in Cortland. In 1960, the Hot Truck appeared on Stewart Avenue, manned by Bob Petrillose, whose family operated Johnny's Big Red Grill. Bob's claim to fame was an original combination of tomato sauce, mozzarella, and toppings on buttered French bread, dubbed "Poor Man's Pizza."

*Factoid*: When C. Alan MacDonald, a graduate of Cornell's School of Hotel Administration, became CEO of the Stouf-fer Food Corporation, one of the new products he intro-duced was inspired by his late night munchies at the Hot Truck. Stouffer's French Bread Pizza became one of the frozen food division's most successful products.

## TRUE DETECTIVE

Abraham Lincoln would never have become President were it not for the detective work of a man born in a log cabin in the Cortland County town of Homer in 1809, the same year Lincoln was born in a log cabin in

83

Hodgeville, Kentucky. Eli DeVoe, a member of the newly formed Secret Service, was involved with thwarting a plot to assassinate the President-elect on February 23, 1861, when Lincoln's train was scheduled to stop in Baltimore while en route to the nation's capital. Ironically, DeVoe would later participate in arresting two of the conspirators in the successful assassination of Lincoln.

*Factoid*: The group planning Lincoln's murder was The Knights of the Golden Circle, a secret society with plans to annex a "golden circle" of territories in Mexico, Central America, the Confederate States of America, and the Caribbean as slave states, to be led by Maximilian I of Mexico.

## SWIMMING LESSONS

Born in Naples, the daughter of New York Governor Myron Clark, Mary Clark was educated in the Ontario Female Seminary in Canandaigua. In 1857 she married Frederick Ferris Thompson, the son of the founder of the 1st National Bank of the City of New York (later Citibank). Although the Thompson's principal residence was 283 Madison Avenue in New York City, the couple spent their summers in Mary's girlhood home in Canandaigua. The estate was named Sonnenberg ("Sunny Hill" in German). In 1885, they tore down the farmhouse and replaced it with a 40-room Queen -Anne style mansion. (In 2005, the New York State Office of Parks, Recreation and Historic Preservation bought the estate and opened the mansion to visitors). Expressing a desire that "every boy and girl in town shall learn to swim;" Mrs. Thompson presented plans for a swimming school in 1905 to be built at the Canandaigua lakefront. It was constructed, funded, and maintained at her expense with competent instructors in charge.

*Factoid*: The original shoreline of Canandaigua Lake is the edge of Lakeshore Drive. The land that now extends 500 feet into the lake is called Kershaw Park, the result of filling in the lake between 1920 and 1936. Lovers of old cars may cringe thinking of the many Model Ts, and other antiques, which were dumped in the lake to anchor the earth and rocks used to make the park. The bathhouse in the park is modeled after the Swimming School that Mary Clark Thompson donated to the city in 1906.

## FIRE DOWN BELOW

The era of steam-propelled excursion boats was a time of enterprise in Finger Lakes history. One of the most famous of the Cayuga Lake steamers was the Frontenac. On July 27, 1907, the Frontenac left Ithaca with forty passengers, Captain Brown, and a crew of five men and one woman. It stopped at Sheldrake and then headed for Aurora in unsteady waters, as Captain Brown reported, "The waves were high and the wind was blowing a gale." A few minutes before 1 PM, a young boy discovered a fire and reported it to his mother. The captain was quickly informed, but his efforts to extinguish the fire proved futile due to the overpowering winds feeding the flames. As some passengers were putting on life preservers, it became clear that they needed to jump into the water and get away from the boat as soon as possible. Strong waves made it difficult for women in their large skirts to make much success in swimming toward shore, a distance of perhaps only 200 feet. Seven women and one boy were drowned.

*Factoid*: The wreckage of the Frontenac remained a curiosity for years after the tragedy. It remained near the Aurora lakeshore until World War II when the demand for scrap iron was so great the wreckage was used for the production of armaments.

## INLAND PORT

While it has sprouted incongruously among the warehouses of Ithaca's West End industrial park, Frédéric Bouché's micro-winery has an historic connection to the neighborhood. The West End was once referred to as "the Rhine," the area's meandering inlet reminiscent of the Rhine River in

Germany. Back in the early 1900s, it was a community of shacks and shanties, where many of the inhabitants were moonshiners and where liquor-making was an essential enterprise. Today, Ports of New York Winery at 815 Taber Street is the first and only winery in the Finger Lakes exclusively devoted to fortified wines that mimic wines from Portugal's Douro region.

*Factoid*: Due to a trade agreement with the European Union, Bouché's wines cannot be called "Port." He calls them "Meleau," from the Latin mel (honey) and the French eau (water).

## WHERE PIES GO WHEN THEY DIE

Virgil is a quiet farming community in the hilly Cortland County countryside that comes alive each autumn, as the rural crafts of apple cider-making and apple pie-baking begin at Hollenbeck's Cider Mill, just as it has ever since 1933. Juice for cider is extracted from a century-old Boomer and Boschert wooden press in a room filled with the scent of glorious, flaky, apple pies. A noisy, mechanical 4-cup peeler cores and peels the green skin, then, in one motion, slices each apple into 16 pieces to make life easy for the bakers. While the exact recipe for Hollenbeck's apple pie is a guarded family secret, the mix of apples includes an heirloom variety called Greening, whose sweet-tart flavor intensifies when heated, just dandy in fresh-out-of-the-oven apple pies.

*Factoid*: It is said that the first Greening seedling was found in 1700 outside a tavern at Green's End in Newport, Rhode Island, then propagated widely throughout the Northeast. This apple was a favorite of Benjamin Franklin for its thin, tender skin, covering a crisp, rich, juicy flesh.

## MONTEZUMA'S REVENGE

Before the Finger Lakes region was settled, there existed a vast wetland north of Cayuga Lake that extended nearly to Lake Ontario, the remnant of a lake formed when the glaciers were melting back into Canada. The name "Montezuma" was first used in 1806 by Dr. Peter Clark for his 12-room estate overlooking the marshes, inspired by his trip to Mexico City and the site of the Aztec Emperor's palace. With a mixture of nutrient-rich waters, lush and diverse vegetation, and rich invertebrate and insect life, the Montezuma Swamp has historically provided a resting, nesting and feeding habitat for waterfowl and other migratory birds on their journeys to and from northeastern Canada. In 1938, President Franklin D. Roosevelt signed Executive Order 7971 which established Montezuma as a refuge for the tens of thousands of birds and fowl that use the swamp as a stop-over along their migratory routes. The 3.5-mile Wildlife Drive which encircles many of the ponds and pools features a local radio station as well as "guide by cell" information points that describes the nature of the refugee, numerous ponds, and the many species of birds that visit the wetland.

*Factoid*: Digging the Erie Canal required extensive work to bypass some natural features. None was greater than the effort to pass through the Montezuma Swamp, where it was rumored that over a thousand people died of malaria during construction.

## INSPIRED BY THE CLASSICS

New York Surveyor-General Simeon DeWitt is often given credit for providing ancient Greek and Roman names to the twenty-eight central Military Tract townships in the Finger Lakes region that his office mapped after the Revolutionary War. In fact, it was Irish-born Robert Harpur, the Deputy Secretary of State and Secretary of the Land Board in the infant New York State government who drew on his background as a University of Glascow-educated classical scholar to suggest names, as request by Dewitt, "that were neither English nor Indian." The names he came up with were: Aurelius, Brutus, Camillus, Cato, Cicero, Cincinnatus, Dryden, Fabius, Galen, Hannibal, Hector, Homer, Junius, Locke, Lysander, Manlius,

Marcellus, Milton, Ovid, Pompey, Romulus, Scipio, Sempronius, Solon, Sterling, Tully, Virgil, and Ulysses. After acquiring a portion of the Ulysses tract at the southern end of Cayuga Lake in 1804, DeWitt called the new town Ithaca, after the island home of Ulysses in Greek mythology.

*Factoid*: Harpursville in Broome County, as well as Harpur College (now Binghamton University) was named for Robert Harpur.

## BIRD IS THE WORD

It was initially a short talk presented together with a Cornell graduate student, Cuthbert Fraser, about a most unusual bird from the Gobi Desert, called a "woofen-poof" by the local populace. A 4-page article detailing the anatomy, ecology and evolution of the Eoornis Pterovelox Gobiensis was subsequently written in the 1920s by Augustus C. Fotheringham, a pseudonym for botanist Lester W. Sharp, the article circulated through scientist circles, handed down with a wink and a nod. Numerous people bought into the story before it was revealed to be an elaborate hoax.

*Factoid*: Known for his wit, Professor Sharp was vice-president of the American Society of Naturalists in 1924, vice-president of the Botanical Society of America in 1929 and president in 1930.

## HAPPY HOUR AT KLAPPROTH'S

The father of American literature and the greatest humorist America has produced, Mark Twain, born Samuel Langhorne Clemens, married Olivia Langdon, member of a prominent Elmira family. He spent more than 20 summers and wrote some of his greatest works in Elmira, while summering with his in-laws on Quarry Farm. The wooden octagon in which Huckleberry Finn and Tom Sawyer were born is open to visitors on the grounds of Elmira College. Twain was known to frequent a now-defunct bar called Klapproth's Tavern in downtown Elmira, where it's said he often could be found after telling his wife that he was going off to "do his banking."

*Factoid*: Mark Twain is buried in Elmira's Woodlawn Cemetery (1200 Walnut Street) with his wife, and their four children. Between 2,000 and 3,000 people visit the grave every year, many of whom leave mementos, including bottles of bourbon and cigars. "I do not fear death," the great man wrote. "I had been dead for billions and billions of years before I was born, and had not suffered the slightest inconvenience from it."

## LEAPING INTO THE UNKNOWN

Cornell University's deep gorges have earned the unwanted distinction of "Suicide Capital of the Ivy League." Although commensurate with national averages, suicide at Cornell, or "gorging out," has become the stuff of myth. Between 1990 and 2010, 29 people attempted suicide by jumping from bridges into Ithaca's gorges. Twenty-seven were successful, 15 of the 27 were Cornell students.

*Factoid*: Cornell installed horizontal nets made of tensile steel mesh underneath six bridges on and near campus and vertical mesh on the suspension bridge. The net systems, extending 15 feet out from the bridges, replaced temporary fences erected after the 2010 suicides.

## FROZEN OCEAN

The land was clear-cup and settled by Irish immigrants fleeing the potato famine in the mid-1800s. Situated on one of the highest points in Cayuga County near Moravia, the elevation (1,620 feet) made farming difficult, so the settlers moved on, and the foundations, wells, and plantings still remain. Today, 754 acres of Frozen Ocean State Forest provide hiking, cross-country skiing, hunting, trapping, camping, and nature viewing along a 1.8 mile out and back trail.

*Factoid*: The area is well known for receiving more than its fair share of freezing winds in the winter, but why it's called Frozen Ocean is a mystery.

## A WINE NAMED CAYUGA

Most hybrid grapes intended for winemaking were developed by French scientists between 1880 and 1950. Their goal was to combine the finer taste characteristics of European vinifera varieties with the winter-hardiness and disease-resistance of the Native-American varieties. Among hybrid varieties developed specifically for the Finger Lakes and other cool climate regions by Cornell University's New York State Agricultural Experiment Station in Geneva, Cayuga White is a mid-season-ripening wine grape from crosses of two other hybrids, Schuyler and Seyval Blanc.

*Factoid*: One of the early success stories of the Cornell Grape Breeding Program, Cayuga White has become one of the most commonly-produced white hybrid varieties in the Finger Lakes. The mother-block of Cayuga White can be found at Cayuga Ridge Estate Winery in Ovid, blanketing 8 acres of the vineyard with vigorous clusters of the greenish-gold, translucent grapes.

## BREAKFAST OF CHAMPIONS

The historic gristmill at New Hope began supplying Finger Lakes kitchens with whole-grain flours in 1823, when Judge Charles Kellogg discovered a unique location along Bear Swamp Creek, just before it empties into Skaneateles Lake. He built a flour mill below a twenty-eight foot waterfall with a dam above that would store water each night to turn the millstones on the following day. New Hope Mills was one of the very first commercial producers of pancake mixes, and the company's signature products include the highest-grade unbleached and unenriched flours, free of chemical additives, blended with baking powder and salt or sugar, according to closely-held formulas, bequeathed from generation to generation. The factory store at 181 York Street in Auburn sells pancake mixes, as well as syrups, spreads, spices and baking supplies.

*Factoid*: Since their humble beginnings in 1797, the Birkett Mills in Penn Yan has not only grown to become one of the largest manufacturers of buckwheat products in the entire world, but has cooked what *The Guinness Book of World Records* confirmed to be the largest buckwheat pancake in history. On Sept. 27, 1987, a cement mixer was hired to mix the batter, poured onto a 28-foot griddle, and flipped by a crane. The griddle now resides on the side of the Birkett Mills building at 1 East Main Street in downtown Penn Yan.

## FOUR SCORE AND SEVEN YEARS AGO

Abraham Lincoln delivered the 272-word Gettysburg Address on November 19, 1963 on the battlefield near Gettysburg, Pennsylvania, where Union and Confederate soldiers fought one of the bloodiest battles of the Civil War. Several months later, historian George Bancroft attended a reception at the White House, where he asked Lincoln for a handwritten copy of the address. That manuscript is now the highlight of Cornell University Library's Division of Rare and Manuscript Collections in Kroch Library on the university campus. It is one of five known copies of the Gettysburg address written and signed by Lincoln himself.

*Factoid*: Cornell's copy of Lincoln's Gettysburg Address is the only copy owned by a private institution. The four other copies are owned by public institutions – two at the Library of Congress, one at the Illinois State Historical Library, and one in the Lincoln Room at the White House.

# TURN LEFT AT CONNECTICUT

Connecticut Hill, located southwest of Ithaca astride the Tompkins-Schuyler County lines, is the largest Wildlife Management Area in New York State. From 1800 to 1879, the tract totaling 11,045 acres was owned by the state of Connecticut and then sold to private landowners. However, the name, Connecticut Hill, stuck. As with many other high grounds in the state, farmers found that it was too great a challenge to grow anything and they were uprooted. During the Great Depression, New York acquired the land through the Federal Resettlement Administration, and it was allowed to reforest.

*Factoid*: During the American colonial era, New York and Connecticut often disputed the precise location of their shared border, leading to a bloodless border war that eventually gave the colonies their modern shapes. Though the dispute was officially resolved in 1731, effects of the boundary conflict persisted until well after both colonies gained statehood following the American Revolution.

# SODOM ON CAYUGA

During its frontier days, one of the nicknames for Ithaca was "Sodom," after the Biblical city of sin, a reputation earned by the town's penchant for horseracing, gambling, profanity, Sabbath breaking, and readily available hooch. With the opening of the Erie Canal and building of the railroads, Ithaca was connected to more of the outside world, and with economic boom came successive waves of gamblers, bootleggers, prostitutes, and con artists, many settling in the rough and rowdy West End. That part of town became known as the "Silent City," since residents would keep quiet when the police came to investigate a reported crime.

*Factoid*: Disrepute was further buoyed by Ithaca's "godless university," a reference to Cornell's lack of affiliation with any organized religion.

# Educated Ice Cream

The Cornell Dairy Bar in Stocking Hall at the corner of Judd Falls and Tower Road on the Cornell University campus is home of "educated ice cream." Inside a classroom-turned-ice cream parlor, students from the food science department devise ways to use milk from the College of Veterinary Medicine-managed herd of 900 cows, crafting premium ice cream flavors in small batches. Students and visitors order up a dish or cone while watching ice cream production in process through a two-story glass wall and an indoor observational balcony.

*Factoid*: Besides vanilla, chocolate, and strawberry, innovative flavors include "Big Red Bear Tracks," named in honor of the Cornell mascot at athletic events, is vanilla ice cream with brownie pieces and a caramel swirl.

# Copper John's Johnson

Being sentenced to the Auburn Correctional Facility used to mean you were "going to work for Copper John." A weird signature of this maximum state prison, the statue of a Revolutionary War soldier standing "on duty" at 135 State Street, Copper John symbolically protects citizens from the inmates. Originally a wooden statue that was erected atop the administration office of the prison in 1821, it had weathered so much that in 1848 it was taken down and a new statue was made out of copper by the prisoners in the prison foundry.

*Factoid*: In 2004, a state government official became aware that the statue was fashioned to be "anatomically correct" and ordered the statue to be "incorrected." Correctional officers passed out T-shirts showing the iconic statue and reading "Save Copper John's Johnson," but the statue was nonetheless removed, and the bulge in his pants was filed down before remounting.

# BACK FROM THE DEAD

Jemima Wilkinson was born on November 29, 1758 in Cumberland, Rhode Island to Quaker parents. When she was twenty-four years old, she fell extremely ill with typhoid fever. On the fifth day of the fever, she became unconscious and appeared to be close to death. When she awoke, Wilkinson declared that she had actually passed through the gates of heaven and had been raised from the dead, reincarnated as a prophet known as the Public Universal Friend, who was neither male nor female. She is called the first American-born woman to found a religious group, also considered a "transgender evangelist." Eventually, Wilkinson and her followers settled in the Finger Lakes, establishing the village they called New Jerusalem, since renamed Penn Yan.

*Factoid*: A two-and-a-half story, framed Federal-style residence at 3912 Friend Hill Road in Penn Yan is the only surviving home of Jemima Wilkinson. Her death in 1819 led directly to the demise of the Society. She was briefly interred in a vault in the cellar of the house and later buried in an unmarked location on the property.

# FROM NEWSBOY TO NEWSPAPER MOGUL

A man who carved out an empire in America's newspaper world was born in 1876 on a small farm in South Bristol, just west of Canandaigua Lake. Frank Ernest Gannett peddled papers as a boy and worked his way through Cornell University as a cub reporter for *The Ithaca Journal*. After graduating in 1898, he became the Journal's managing editor, business manager, and by 1912, its owner. In 1918, he bought two Rochester newspapers and by the end of the 1920, owned 15 dailies in New York and other papers in New Jersey, Connecticut and Illinois. Active in politics, Gannett arrived in Philadelphia with three circus elephants to attend the 1940 Republican Convention but lost his bid for the presidential nomination to corporate lawyer Wendell Wilkie. During his lifetime, Frank Gannett amassed a publishing group of 22 newspapers in 18 cities. He owned four radio stations and three television stations. Today, the company is the country's largest newspaper group with 95 daily newspapers, including national publication *USA Today*. Among his philanthropic gifts, Gannett donated half a million dollars for the construction of the Gannett Health Center at Cornell.

*Factoid*: Older than *The New York Times*, Ithaca's daily newspaper, *The Ithaca Journal*, traces its origin to publisher Jonathan Ingersoll and his Seneca Republican, its first issue printed on Independence Day, 1815. When the *Journal* was purchased by Frank Gannett in 1912, it was only the second newspaper in what would eventually become the Gannett media conglomerate.

## *FLYBOY*

The first air show in America was held on a field in Pleasant Valley (near Hammondsport) on July 4, 1908 when native son Glenn H. Curtiss, holder of Pilot's License No. 1, flew his aircraft named the "June Bug" for one mile up the valley in front of hundreds of spectators. The next year, he flew the "Golden Flyer" a distance of 24.7 miles to establish a world distance record. Curtiss was called the "Fastest Man on Earth" after reaching a speed of 136.4 miles per hour on his motorcycle in Orlando, Florida. He also built the very first "travel trailer" in 1917, a luxury fifth wheel trailer complete with a toilet, kitchenette, Pullman-style beds, and a built in radio.

*Factoid*: The Glenn H. Curtiss Museum at 8419 Route 54 outside the village of Hammondsport, a veritable Smithsonian of early flight and experimentation, concentrates on his life, time and accomplishments, showcasing 25 full-sized aircraft, countless bicycles and motorcycles in a 57,000 sq. foot former wine warehouse.

# THE BEST OF THE WEST IN THE EAST

The most comprehensive collection of Western art east of the Mississippi is housed in the Rockwell Museum of Western Art in Corning. In 1980 the museum was moved from the Baron Steuben Hotel to the city's old city hall (built in 1893) on 111 Cedar Street. The Rockwell's wide-ranging collection covers classic Americana and cowboy scenes, as well as more contemporary work by Native American artists and others. In 2015, the museum was named a Smithsonian Affiliate, the first in New York State outside of New York City.

*Factoid*: The museum is named after local art collector Bob Rockwell, no relation to Norman Rockwell, however, the collection does include one Norman Rockwell piece, "The Buffalo Hunt."

# COLLABORATION WITH NATURE

The site-specific artworks of Andy Goldsworthy, British sculptor and photographer, directly engage with the environment, incorporating natural specimens and found objects into semi-permanent sculptures, which are then documented in photographs. Goldsworthy produced numerous ephemeral works on the Cornell University campus, along Fall Creek gorge, in 1999 and 2000, using brilliant red and golden leaves. However, his mound of rough locally-quarried stones on the Hoyt-Pileated Trail in the Sapsucker Woods Sanctuary, constructed in 2008, is a permanent installation.

*Factoid*: Four replacement boulders for Goldworthy's Garden of Stone installation are on indefinite loan from the Museum of Jewish Heritage in New York City, and can be found at the east end of the F. R. Newman Arboretum in the Cornell Plantations. The chestnut oak trees growing from the large boulders stand as a living memorial to the Holocaust.

# COMPULSORY PATRIOTISM

Banners around Mount Morris, in Livingston County, west of Conesus Lake, proclaim the town as "Birthplace of Francis Bellamy," the Baptist minister who wrote the Pledge of Allegiance for the opening ceremonies of the Columbian Exposition in October 1892, the 400th anniversary of Christopher Columbus' arrival in the New World. A key element of the commemorative program was a new salute to the flag for schoolchildren to recite in unison. By the time of the Second World War, many states had made the daily recitation of the pledge mandatory for teachers and students.

*Factoid*: Originally, the pledge was begun with the right hand over the heart, and after reciting, the arm was extended toward the flag, palm-down. In World War II, the salute too much resembled the Nazi salute, so it was changed to keep the right hand over the heart throughout

# GHOST WINERY

No winery property in the Finger Lakes has more interesting history than Miles Wine Cellars in Himrod on Seneca Lake. Originally a land-grant from the King of England to the Rapalee family, its dock on Seneca Lake provided area farmers with access to the barges that moved their produce to the cities. An imposing house, built in 1802, was originally Federal -style in design, then converted to Greek Revival fifty years later by the Rapalees. It became a stop on the Underground Railroad, a shelter for runaway slaves as they made their way north and into Canada where they could live as free citizens. But what makes this place even more interesting are the strange noises, unexplained events, and actual sightings of ghosts. Current owners – the Miles family – hired a clairvoyant to confirm that as many as seven spirits are wandering the farm.

*Factoid*: The winery produces a proprietary blend of Chardonnay and

Cayuga grapes for a wine called "Ghost," picturing two of the spirits who reside in the mansion.

## MOUNDBUILDERS

The earliest inhabitants of the territory around Owasco Lake were the Native American Alleghans who constructed the Osco Mound over several acres within what is now the city of Auburn, just west of downtown and one block south of Genesee Street. They built an earthen altar for the worship of the sun within the walls of the fortress and mounds for the burial of their dead outside the walls. Because of its height and strategic location, the Mound was viewed by European settlers as a fortress, and it was called "Fort Hill." In 1851, most of the land occupied by the Mound was sold for $1 to a cemetery association, and the archaeological treasure became a graveyard. Fort Hill Cemetery was consecrated on July 7, 1852. Buried there are William Seward, Lincoln's Secretary of State and Captain Myles W. Keogh, who died alongside Lieutenant Colonel Custer at the Battle of the Little Bighorn.

*Factoid*: In 1853, the Cemetery Association completed construction of a 56-foot-high obelisk of native limestone in memory of Logan, Chief of the Cayugas. On the north side of the memorial, an inscription reads: "Who is there to mourn for Logan?"

## TALLER THAN NIAGARA

Taughannock Falls is the tallest single-drop waterfalls in the Northeast. Its 215-foot vertical drop – 33 feet longer than iconic Niagara Falls – plunges through a rock amphitheater whose walls reach nearly 400 feet. Dense spray rising from the bottom of the glen often shrouds the lower part of the cataract in mist. Legend has it that the falls are named for a Delaware Indian chief who, upon leading his tribe to invade the local Cayuga people, was thrown from the top of the cliff to his demise in the pools below. A 600-acre estate, once owned by Philadelphian John Jones, from the falls stretching to the edge of Cayuga Lake, was deeded to New York State in the 1930s, creating Taughannock Falls State Park.

*Factoid*: In 1874, Canadian daredevil Andrew Jenkins, professionally known as "The Professor," traversed Taughannock gorge on a four-inch diameter rope 1,200 feet long, pedaling a vehicle resembling an upside-down bicycle with wooden wheels with deep grooves so the rope would fit inside them – a feat he had performed 4 years earlier over Niagara Falls.

## WORSHIP AT TIFFANY'S

After the death of John Davenport in 1895, his brother Ira, Jr. hired the Tiffany Glass Company in New York City to install a stained-glass sanctuary for the Presbyterian Church in Bath in his memory. Completed in 1887, the wall-to-wall, floor-to-ceiling design was the work of Louis Comfort Tiffany. Jacob Wrey Mould, a British architect, illustrator, linguist and musician, was noted for his contributions to the design and construction of New York City's Central Park. The Presbyterian Church in Bath is the only remaining church designed by Mould.

*Factoid*: Built in 1892 to 1894, Willard Chapel in Auburn is a hidden treasure, its interior designed and constructed by Louis Comfort Tiffany. The chapel is the only complete and unaltered totally Tiffany-designed religious interior known to exist in the world.

## SKY'S THE LIMIT

On clear Friday nights, visitors to the Cornell University campus in Ithaca come to view the moon, planets, galaxies, and star clusters through the century-old Fuertes Observatory's telescope. Fuertes was completed in the fall of 1917 and its main instrument, the Irving Porter Church Telescope, followed in October 1922. The building honors Estevan A. Fuertes, professor of Civil Engineering, and later Dean of the engineering school. The telescope, a historic 12-inch refractor, still driven by the original mechanical clockwork mechanism, honors Irving Porter Church, professor and chair of the Department of Civil Engineering. The observatory is also home to equipment used in the 19th century for geodesy and timekeeping, which is on display in a museum occupying the east wing of the building.

*Factoid*: Fuertes is no longer used for professional research; observational classes and research are conducted instead at the Hartung-Boothroyd Observatory atop Mount Pleasant in Ithaca.

## SIGN OF THE TIMES

One of the largest and oldest continually operating breweries in the United States, the Genesee Brewing Company of Rochester makes Genesee Beer, Genny Light, and Genesee Cream Ale. In 1952, the company installed a giant billboard in the city of Auburn. The iconic sign, 26 feet high and 48 feet wide, found its place atop the six-story building then called Auburn Music Center (later Speno Music) at 3 East Genesee Street. Standing 85 feet from the ground to the top, the sign has become a central fixture of downtown Auburn.

*Factoid*: In 2011, Genesee retrofitted the iconic sign with 9,000 state-of-the-art LED lights, inside of 380-feet of rope, replacing the original neon tubes. Today, the Genesee Beer sign automatically turns on at dusk and turns off at dawn.

## THIRST FOR KNOWLEDGE

It's the hardest class to get into at Cornell University. HADM 4300, Introduction to Wines, is a wine tasting course taught in the Hotel School's Alice Statler Auditorium. Students who are lucky enough to register receive college credit while swirling, sniffing, and sipping wines from around the world. During each once-a-week, two-hour class, students learn about six or seven wines. They study (and are tested on) the characteristics of the region (including climate and soil properties), the wine's vineyard, producer, grape qualities and every aspect of the label.

*Factoid*: Founded in 1922, the Cornell School of Hotel Administration was the world's first four-year intercollegiate school devoted to hospitality management.

## THEY SHOOT HORSES, DON'T THEY?

In a centuries-old practice, military forces used packhorses to carry baggage and provisions. The first large-scale use of packhorses by Continental forces was Major General John Sullivan's army 1779 campaign against the Iroquois Confederacy. Union quartermasters purchased Morgans, a uniquely American breed known for stamina, versatility, heart and courage, but after the long trek, and the weight on the packhorses unrelenting, by the time they returned through Elmira, they had reached the end of their endurance. Sullivan was forced to mercifully dispose of a large number of sick and disabled horses. Remaining Iroquois collected the skulls and arranged them in a line along the trail. That spot, from that time forward was referred to as the "valley of the horse's heads," today the town of Horseheads.

*Factoid*: Horseheads is the first and only town and village in the United States dedicated to the service of the American Military Horse. A twenty-eight square mile memorial, unparalleled in American military hstory, enshrines the town of Horseheads, the only town in the United States dedicated to the service of the American military horse. A military packhorse statue, dedicated in May of 2013, stands near the village hall.

## RED INSTEAD

At Shalestone Vineyards in Hector, winemaker Rob Thomas has achieved stature in the region and a loyal following with the mantra, "Red is all we do," a symbol of artistic individualism and a unique niche among the region's mostly white wine producers. Rob handcrafts 10,000 bottles of red wine varietals and creative blends each year, including a Lemberger-Merlot-Syrah proprietary blend cheekily called "Lemberghini." His rich, concentrated beauties are as close as we come to cult wines in the Finger Lakes.

*Factoid*: The winery's name was inspired by a site where vine roots have barely 12 inches of soil above layers of fractured shale (or shale bedrock), deposited by ancient glaciers.

## AMERICA'S FIRST RAP STARS

Kate and Maggie Fox grew up in Hydesville (now Arcadia) in Wayne County. As young girls, they began to hear "rappings" they believed were communications from spirits. In formal séances the sisters developed a code in which rap sounds would signify yes or no in response to a question posed to the "other world." In 1850 they embarked on a professional tour to spread word of the spirits, while an editorial in the Scientific American scoffed at their claims, calling the girls the "Spiritual Knockers from Rochester." Horace Greeley, the prominent publisher and politician, became a kind of protector for them, enabling their movement in higher social circles. They also attracted imitators, and during the following few years, hundreds of people claimed the ability to communicate with spirits.

*Factoid*: The Fox sisters were routinely exposed by skeptics as fakes and it was claimed they produced their phenomena with ventriloquism or mechanical devices. In 1888, Margaret and Kate confessed that their strange rappings had been a hoax and publicly demonstrated their method of simply cracking their toe joints.

## HIGHER EDUCATION

The Town of Macedon in Wayne County is named after the birthplace of Alexander the Great in ancient Greece.  In pioneer days, a small tavern known as the Hollister House stood on the northwest corner of Macedon Center and did a thriving business, that is, until the Erie Canal was opened and most travelers came into the region by water route.  In 1841 the tavern became the first home of the Macedon Academy, a co-ed private institution founded by Quakers as a place of not only intermediate academic education, its curriculum governed by strict rules, sometimes locally termed "Blue Laws."  In an era when most district schools taught only up to the eighth grade, the academy's mission was roughly the equivalent of today's high schools.  Its outstanding curriculum and reputation attracted students throughout the Finger Lakes and beyond.  The last graduating class was held at the Academy in 1902, after the State refused to continue aid to the school.

*Factoid*:  First erected in Macedon in 1858, the Aldrich Change Bridge is the oldest iron bridge in New York State and one of only two bridges known to survive from the first enlargement of the Erie Canal.

## OUT WITH THE OLD, IN WITH THE NEW

The twin 14-story residential towers on Ithaca College's South Hill campus have a commanding presence above the city, and since 1965 they have provided Ithacans a ceremo-nial light show to usher in the New Year.  The tradition be-gan as the brainchild of Petrus Van de Velde, former Assistant Supervisor of Custodial Services at the college.  For a few days before the holiday, lights in mapped-out windows of the towers are illumi-nated to spell out the cur-rent calendar year in 100-foot-high numerals.

At the stroke of midnight on New Year's Eve, the towers' fire alarms are sounded as a signal, and in precisely co-ordinated teamwork, lights are turned on and off in the pre-determined rooms, instantly adjusting the display to mark the dawn of the New Year with its new number. Ithaca's version of the Times Square ball drop is a dramatic scene against the nighttime sky, visible for miles around.

*Factoid*: Special fixtures, originally with 300-watt incandescent bulbs (now with 100-watt fluorescents), are placed in the windows of student rooms (vacant over the holidays), and connected on each floor to a single power source, manned by as many as 25 volunteers from the college staff.

## THE GREAT AGNOSTIC

In the late 19th century, new and bold ideas from Europe, including biblical criticism and the theories of Charles Darwin, challenged traditional ways of thinking about religion. Among the most controversial characters in America, Robert Green Ingersoll abandoned belief in God and became known among his admirers as "the Great Agnostic." Born to a Presbyterian pastor and ardent abolitionist in the Yates County village of Dresden, on August 11, 1833, Ingersoll devastatingly dissected a wide array of biblical absurdities, including a day-by-day postmortem of the seven days of creation. The Robert Green Ingersoll Birthplace Museum at 61 Main Street in Dresden showcases his power as a persuader and his role in history.

*Factoid*: Ingersoll enjoyed a friendship with Walt Whitman, who considered Ingersoll the greatest orator of his time. Upon Whitman's death during 1892, Ingersoll delivered the eulogy at the poet's funeral.

## SCHOOL SPIRIT

Sage Chapel, a non-denominational house of worship on the Cornell University campus, was erected in 1874, the gift of Henry W. Sage, an early benefactor and trustee of the university. Originally buried at Lake View Cemetery, Ezra Cornell's remains were moved to the memorial antechapel in Sage Chapel and sealed in an ornate, white marble sarcophagus designed by sculptor William Wetmore Story. Sage Chapel is a popular choice for couples getting married at Cornell, and the bride traditionally uses the antechapel to prepare, as no other appropriate room exists. Many believe the spirit of Ezra Cornell rises to bless the marriages.

*Factoid*: Cornell, founded as a nonsectarian university, was often attacked by its detractors for its lack of religious emphasis, earning itself the nickname "the heathens on the hill" or "infidel Cornell." Sage Chapel was the first voluntary chapel at an American university.

## HARD TO SWALLOW

Among the strangest and most bizarre dishes served in the Finger Lakes, the "Pig's Plate" is a version of the Rochester-born, inelegantly-named "garbage plate" offered at Seneca Farms, just south of Penn Yan on Route 54A. The over-the-top concoction includes choice of hotdog or cheeseburger stacked on top of macaroni salad, baked beans and French fries, then smothered in chili, ketchup and mustard.

*Factoid*: In 1950, Seneca Farms became the first drive-thru restaurant in the Finger Lakes.

## THE PUMP THAT ROARED

The first all-metal pump in the world was cast and assembled in a little stone shop at Green and Ovid Streets in Seneca Falls by Seabury S. Gould's manufacturing company. Gould's Pumps became the world's largest pump manufacturer (acquired by ITT Technology in 1997). Norman Judd Gould, the grandson of the founder, was the company's fourth President and the last member of the Gould family to serve in management of the company.

He guided the company through periods of vast changes in technologies and products. Construction of a red brick, four-story hotel on Fall Street in Seneca Falls began in 1919, named the Gould Hotel after Norman Gould, its main financier. In 1920, *The Syracuse Journal* claimed the Gould Hotel to be "the most complete and perfectly equipped of the smaller hotels of New York State."

*Factoid*: At one time, Seneca Falls had the highest per capita level of industrialization of any place in New York State, and the highest concentration of millionaires of any community in the United States.

## EVICTION NOTICE, BY GEORGE

In September of 1779, under the personal orders of George Washington, Major General John Sullivan's army engaged in a systematic military campaign against tribes of the Iroquois Confederacy who had sided with the British. Sullivan's army carried out a scorched earth campaign, methodically destroying at least forty Indian villages throughout the Finger Lakes region, as terrified families escaped to Canada seeking protection of the British. The word "Coreorgonel" translates to "where we keep the pipe of peace," the name for an area near Buttermilk Falls in Ithaca, where members of the Tutelo tribe had settled in 1753. The Tutelos managed to flee before Sullivan's army arrived on September 24, 1779. Most trekked 120 miles to Fort Niagara, seeking refuge at the British stronghold, while many starved or froze to death in harsh early winter conditions.

*Factoid*: Tutelo Park, just off Bostwick Road in Ithaca, commemorates Ithaca's original inhabitants with wooded nature trails and native wildflower plantings. It has the county's largest shagbark hickory and black oak trees, and is home to many species of wild birds.

# SLICE OF AMERICANA

Dating all the way back to 1849, the general store in the Steuben County hamlet of North Cohocton was the place to go for everyday needs and the chance to get the latest local gossip. First operated by the Wetmore Brothers, in 1898 it was sold to Henry Wolfanger and Henry Pierce. They named the store Wolfanger & Pierce, but it was lovingly called "The Two Hanks." Henry Wolfanger was sole owner after Henry Pierce died, and in 1951, Charles and Marion Briglin took over as Briglin's Olde Country Store. The store passed through owner after owner before purchase by the Wells family in 2015. The surviving Olde Country Store now sells honey, maple syrup, mustard, pancake mixes, granola, jams and jellies, cheeses, bulk candies, and a smattering of Finger Lakes merchandise. Over the years, the store's upstairs was used for church groups, political meetings, plays, concerts, roller-skating, lectures, dances, ice cream socials, holiday celebrations, and meetings of Civil War veterans.

*Factoid*: In 1875, William Phelps opened a general store at 140 Market Street in Palmyra and began selling wares delivered on barges crossing the Erie Canal. His son Julius subsequently locked the doors in 1940, leaving a curious retail time capsule of Palmyra in the nineteenth and twentieth centuries.

# THE HOLY OUTLAW

A Jesuit priest, Father Daniel Berrigan emerged in the decade of the 1960s as one of the nation's most influential peace activists, landing him on the Federal Bureau of Investigation's "most wanted list" (the first-ever priest on the list), on the cover of *Time* magazine, and in prison. On May 17, 1968, Berrigan and his brother Philip, along with seven other Catholic protesters, used homemade napalm to destroy 378 draft files in the parking lot of the Catonsville, Maryland draft board. After going into hiding, he was eventually arrested and imprisoned at the Federal Correctional Institution in Danbury, Connecticut until his release on February 24, 1972. Then on September 9, 1980, Berrigan and seven others trespassed onto the General Electric nuclear missile facility in King of Prussia, Pennsylvania, where they damaged nuclear warhead nose cones and poured blood onto documents and files. Their sentences of 1 1/2 to 5 years for some defendants and 3 to 10 years for others were thrown out on the grounds that the trial judge had been biased.

*Factoid*: Father Berrigan served as the Catholic Chaplain at Cornell University in Ithaca from 1966 to 1970, during which time he played an instrumental role in the national peace movement.

## REBEL WITH A CAUSE

Margaret Higgins Sanger was born in Corning on September 14, 1879, one of eleven children of Michael and Anne Higgins. She watched her mother grow weaker with each pregnancy, eighteen in all, and came to believe that in order for women to have a more equal footing in society and to lead healthier lives, they needed to be able to determine when to bear children. In 1916, she opened America's first birth control clinic in Brooklyn, staffed entirely with female doctors. In 1921, Sanger founded the American Birth Control League, which became the Planned Parenthood Federation of America. After separating from her husband in 1914, Sanger, who believed in sexual liberation, began an affair with H.G. Wells. It was at that time she published her first issue of *The Woman Rebel,* a magazine for radical feminists who advocated the right to practice birth control.

*Factoid*: Due to her connection with Planned Parenthood, many who oppose abortion frequently condemn Sanger by criticizing her views on birth control. In spite of such controversies, Sanger continues to be regarded as a force in the American reproductive rights movement and women's rights movement.

## LIKE REGULAR CAMPING, BUT NICER

Combine the experience of camping but with the many of the comforts of a hotel stay, and you have "glamping," short for glamorous camping. The first luxury tent-living enterprise in the Finger Lakes, Firelight Camps at 1150 Danby Road in Ithaca provides safari tents with hardwood flooring, mesh screening, king or queen beds, and battery powered lantern lights. There is an afternoon "wine hour" with Finger Lakes wines, and breakfast is cooked over a communal campfire.

*Factoid*: Even with all these luxuries, if sleeping outdoors is not your cup of tea, you can check into La Tourelle Hotel right next door.

## CHURCHES ON EVERY CORNER

The Wayne County village was originally called Swift's Landing, named for founder John Swift in 1790, and renamed Palmyra after the ancient city in Syria. Citizens of Palmyra provided safe houses along a secret underground railroad route, helping over 2,000 fugitive slaves to escape from the American South into Canada. Palmyra is the only city or village in America to have four churches at a four corner intersection facing each other, and is one of only ten places in the world that has four churches on the four corners of two intersecting highways. The "four corners" churches are at the intersection of Route 21 and Route 31.

*Factoid*: Palmyra was the home of Joseph Smith, the founder of the Church of Jesus Christ of Latter-day Saints, known as the Mormon Church. The Hill Cumorah Pageant, depicting the story of *The Book of Mormon* is an annual production staged at the foot of a 110-foot drumlin in Palmyra.

## BIRDS DO IT

The popularity of soaring in the Chemung River Valley owes a great deal to the geography and topography of the area. With its majestic hills and deep valleys, the updraft from its ridge provides Harris Hill the perfect environment for engineless aircraft, using naturally occurring currents of rising air to remain airborne. At the outbreak of World War II, the Big Flats site was chosen for a glider program, training pilots for the war effort. Today, the Harris Hill Soaring Corporation offers 15 to 20 minute glider rides to brave members of the public.

*Factoid*: The sport of gliding only emerged after the World War I, as a result of the Treaty of Versailles, which imposed severe restrictions on German aircraft manufacture. So while aviators and aircraft makers in the rest of the world were working to improve the performance of powered aircraft, the Germans were designing, developing and flying ever more efficient gliders and discovering ways of using the natural forces in the atmosphere to make them fly farther and faster.

## GODFATHER OF CRAFT COFFEE

The "third wave of coffee" is a movement to produce high-quality coffee and consider coffee an artisanal foodstuff, like fine wine, rather than a commodity. This involves improvements at all stages of production, from coffee growing, harvesting, and processing, to stronger relationships between coffee growers, traders, and roasters, to higher quality and fresh roasting, at times called "microroasting," to skilled brewing. Founded in Ithaca in 2000, Gimme! Coffee has been at the leading edge of the third wave, forming relationships with farmers, using sustainable practices through every step of the supply chain, and elevating coffee above mere drinkability.

*Factoid*: The original Gimme! coffee shop is located at 430 North Cayuga Street in Ithaca. Other locations include 228 Mott Street in Manhattan and 495 Lorimer Street in Brooklyn.

# Road Well Traveled

Routes 5 & 20 had their start as the foot trails of Native Americans hundreds of years before the American Revolution. In the late 1700s, pioneers moving into Central New York, the Finger Lakes region, and the Niagara Frontier widened the footpaths to accommodate their wagons. With the advent of the automobile, these roads were modernized and took on the current designations of Routes 5 and 20, as part of the 3,365 mile transcontinental Federal Highway that connected Boston, Massachusetts to Newport, Oregon. Routes 5 & 20 merge into a single road from Avon, north of Conesus (the westernmost Finger Lake) to Auburn, north of Owasco (the easternmost Finger Lake).

*Factoid*: As the routes proceed across the state, they also directly or indirectly meet every major north to south highway in upstate New York.

# The Postman's Retreat

Gideon Granger was instrumental in helping Thomas Jefferson obtain the office of President in a highly contested and extremely confusing election. His running mate, Aaron Burr, very nearly beat him to the presidency. Beholden to Granger, Jefferson appointed him Postmaster General in 1801, and he served at that post until 1814 when Jefferson's successor, James Madison, replaced him. He remains America's longest serving Postmaster General. Upon leaving Madison's cabinet, Granger moved to Canandaigua, where he would resume his law practice, take up land speculation, and serve one term as a state senator.

*Factoid*: Granger ended his days as a country squire in Canandaigua, resolving to build a home "unrivaled in all the nation." The wood-frame, three-story Granger Homestead at 295 North Main Street is representative of the Federal style of architecture that dominated the landscape in early America.

# LADY OF THE CASTLE

In 1886, Carrie M. Harron, wife of a Manhattan banker, purchased property just south of Geneva, then known as "Bellehurst" (beautiful forest). After divorcing her husband, she married Captain Louis Dell Collins and began building a lavish private residence at 4069 West Lake Road. Fifty men worked for more than four years on the Romanesque-style castle. Mrs. Collins' prize possession was a pair of Japanese Golden Pheasants, often seen roaming the grounds. She left the home to her grandson, who sold it to Cornelius J. "Red" Dwyer, an entrepreneur who turned it into a club and gambling casino. During Prohibition, the club's liquor supply was run down from Canada using the canal system. Duane Reeder bought the property in 1992 and converted Belhurst into a hotel with two restaurant, two ballrooms, a spa, and a wine shop.

*Factoid*: Although she was an independent woman, Carrie was anti-suffrage, so it's interesting that another of her buildings, the Collins Music Hall (now the Elks Club building at 459 South Main Street in Geneva) was host to the 29th New York State (Suffrage) Convention of 1897.

# CULTURED PEARL

Serial films were a staple of the silent movie era, and Pearl White was the queen of the genre. In the classic 1915 series, *The Perils of Pauline*, moviegoers flocked to theaters week after week to see Pearl tied to railroad tracks, threatened by an approaching buzz saw or helplessly drowning in freezing water. They were delighted when she miraculously averted disaster in the next episode. In 1915, she was engaged in filming *The Romance of Elaine*, the follow-up to *The Exploits of Elaine* and *The New Exploits of Elaine,* at the Wharton Brothers' Renwick Park studio in Ithaca. During a break in the filming, Pearl bought a new yellow Stutz Bearcat which became her passion. She was a familiar sight in and around Ithaca as she zoomed through the countryside in her Stutz.

*Factoid*:  In nearby Trumansburg, Ms. White was fined five dollars for speeding.  Instead, she paid ten dollars, and told the village peace justice, "I'm leaving your goddamned town as fast as I came in!"

## THE NAUHEIM TREATMENT

In a search for oil on a hillside property above Seneca Lake in Watkins Glen, drillers went down to a depth of 1,600 feet, and what they found was mineral-laden water, not oil.  Although drillers were disappointed, the water was found to have healing and curative properties, similar to the mineral waters of Nauheim Springs in Germany, the leading spa of the day. The Glen Springs Sanitarium was developed at the site by William E. Leffingwell, attracting guests from around the country and abroad.  Different springs were found to have different properties.  Some provided running water throughout the hotel, while others were used for bathing.  The medical staff treated patients suffering from gout, rheumatism, and digestive problems.  Residents paid $25 to $35 a week to stay at the resort in 1900.

*Factoid*:  When World War II erupted, clientele stopped coming to Glen Springs and it closed in 1942.  The building housed married students attending Cornell University from 1946 through 1948.  In 1949 the Franciscan Friars opened St. Anthony's of Padua Preparatory School, but closed it in 1970.  Next, the Glen Springs Academy, a private boarding school, ran for four years until 1974.  Finally in the early months of 1996, the buildings were demolished.

## THE DRIVE-IN THAT TIME FORGOT

The heyday of drive-ins may be decades in the past, but drive-in culture still flourishes west of the village of Waterloo at Mac's Drive-In at 1166 Waterloo-Geneva Road (Routes 5 & 20).  Since 1961, when the juke box played "Let's Twist Again," the MacDougal family has faithfully maintained car-hop service from a menu which includes hamburgers, French fries, and "chicken-in-a-basket" washed down with root beer and milkshakes. The ice cream window offers sundaes and banana splits.

*Factoid*: The drive-in concept was first popularized by a Texas chain of eateries called the Pig Stand, whose first drive-in opened on a highway connecting Dallas and Fort Worth in 1921. Customers would pull in to the parking lot and be immediately greeted by carhops who served burgers and fries on trays that clipped on to the car's window.

## RIPE FOR THE PICKING

In 1927, Maurice Grisamore quit his conductor's job with the New York Central Railroad, uprooted his family from Chicago, and settled on his newly-purchased farm in the Cayuga County town of Locke. In 1939, the Grisamores began planting strawberries and by 1941, they had an acre of berries, enough to sell to Atwater's grocery store in Ithaca, as well as to passers-by from their front porch. In 1952, with the biggest crop to date and no way to get it all harvested, they advertised "pick-your-own" strawberries, and today, picking in the ripe strawberry fields at Grisamore Farms has become an annual early summer tradition for many families in the region. Thirty acres of strawberries, or nearly two million individual plants, grow on raised beds, and each of the farm's three varieties has been chosen for its peculiarities which include ripening time, resistance to disease, shelf life, color, size, and taste.

*Factoid*: In 1972, heavy rains flooded the farm and the Grisamore's strawberry crop floated away. Without income from strawberries, they planted broccoli, cauliflower, cabbage, and 25 acres of blueberry bushes. In 1975 they planted an apple orchard, and three years later, both sweet and sour cherries.

# Remembering the Fallen

Henry Carter Welles, a prominent druggist in Waterloo, would probably be forgotten today except for a comment that he made to townspeople in the summer of 1865. At a social gathering he suggested that a day should be set aside to honor soldiers killed during the Civil War. The following year, Welles, along with General John B. Murray, commander of the 148th Regiment of New York State Volunteers, gained the support of the village, and on May 5, 1866, the first observance of Memorial Day took place in Waterloo. Memorial Day is often misunderstood as a day to honor troops currently serving in the military. Rather, as the name suggests, it's a day for remembering and honoring those who sacrificed their lives in battle.

*Factoid*: In longstanding tradition, soldiers decorated graves of their fallen comrades with flowers, flags and wreaths, and borrowing on the practice, the observance was sometimes called Decoration Day. Although Memorial Day became its official title in the 1880s, the holiday didn't legally become Memorial Day until 1967.

# The 30-Mile Rule

On Saturday, August 18, 1973, a contingent of agrarians and craftspeople pulled their trucks and station wagons onto an empty lot at Fulton Street near the Agway Farm Store in Ithaca. Some displayed goods on the tailgates of vehicles, others under a patchwork formation of canvas tents and makeshift tables. From this humble endeavor, the Ithaca Farmers Market was born. Today, this nationally-known temple of ultra-locavorism comes alive in a whirlwind of open-air commerce at Steamboat Landing on the Cayuga Lake waterfront, as folks shop for local produce, dairy products, farm-fresh eggs, baked goods and more. Vendors who apply to join the market are required to have offerings juried by a committee of their peers, to whom localness and community are important. Besides rigorous "grow-your-own" standards, every item offered for sale must be grown, produced, or crafted within 30 miles of the Market.

*Factoid*: The popularity of local farmers markets stems from the idea of "food miles," which identifies the distance that food travels from production to sales sites. Buying locally supports the farmer who grows varieties best-suited to local climate and soils, allowing flavor and nutrition to take precedence over transportability. Shorter food miles greatly reduces fossil fuel use and pollution.

## ON THE CLOCK

In 1868, Willard Legrand Bundy opened a jewelry store in Auburn, and as a prolific inventor, he obtained patents for several mechanical devices. However, the invention which made him famous was a time recorder which recorded when workers clocked in and out of work. Before Bundy's invention, a full-time salaried employee would record the comings and goings of workers, notating their names and physically recording in and out times. The timeclock became an integral part of factory environment, allowing supervisors to track the hours of their employees and increasing work place efficiency. In 1890, Bundy moved to Binghamton where he began producing time clocks with his brother as the Bundy Manufacturing Company.

*Factoid*: The clock became so popular, the phrases "to Bundy in" and "Bundy out" became synonymous with clocking in or punching out on the job.

## AMELIA EARHART LANDED HERE

In another life, Ithaca's Hangar Theatre at 801 Taughannock Boulevard was a two-story glass, steel, and stone hangar that served Ithaca Municipal Airport, the first airport in Ithaca and the second airport in New

York State, visited by Amelia Earhart who flew in during a lecture tour supporting sales of her autobiography. Its single short runway, proximity to the Lehigh Valley freight yards on the south side, lake marshes on the north side, and fog in the lake valley posed limits to growth, and in 1948, Cornell University opened the Ithaca Tompkins Regional Airport on East Hill, transferring own-ership to the county in 1956.

*Factoid*: With a grant from politician and philanthropist Nelson Rockefeller, the abandoned airport hangar was renovated in 1975 to become the home of the Center for the Arts at Ithaca. The inaugural season of the Hangar Theatre opened with a production of *Man of La Mancha*.

## WHEN IN ROME

In 1914, Byron Nester, who inherited the fortune his father made by processing barley into malt for the brewing industry, modeled Nester House, his mansion just south of Geneva on Seneca Lake, after Villa Lancellotti, a 16th-century villa he admired on a visit to Rome. The U-shaped structure was built of brick and concrete block and coated in stucco, its interior appointed with Italian marble fireplaces, tapestries, Ionic columns and wood-coffered ceilings. In 1949, the Capuchin Order acquired the villa and operated the Immaculate Heart of Mary Seminary on the property. In 1973, the Capuchins sold the property and it remained vacant for several years. In 1981, Geneva on the Lake was opened as a boutique hotel.

*Factoid*: The Audi family, owners of L. & J.G. Stickley, purchased the resort in 1995 and furnished all 29 guest rooms with Stickley furniture.

## FIRST BREAKFAST CEREAL

James Caleb Jackson was born in the Onondaga County town of Manlius. Troubled with ill health throughout his life, Jackson saw a remarkable recovery after taking a "water cure" at a spa. As a result, he spent the second half of his life as an advocate for hydropathy, training to become a physician and opening a hydropathic institute on Skaneateles Lake. Along with the water cures, Jackson believed that diet was fundamental in improving health. Over time, he removed red meat from the menu at the spa, and ruled out tea, coffee, alcohol and tobacco. He promoted a near-vegetarian diet with the emphasis on fruits, vegetables, and unprocessed grains. In 1863, at the Our Home Hygienic Institute at Dansville, he developed a breakfast cereal he named "Granula," consisting primarily of bran-rich Graham flour rolled into sheets and baked. The dried sheets were then broken into pieces, baked again, and broken into smaller pieces.

*Factoid*: A similar breakfast cereal developed by John Harvey Kellogg at the Battle Creek Sanitarium in Battle Creek, Michigan, was renamed "Granola" to avoid being sued by Jackson.

## THE BIG DITCH

It was America's first great technical innovation. In 1810, New York City Mayor Dewitt Clinton, began promoting the idea of a canal to connect the Great Lakes to the Hudson River, a project he believed would build his city into an economic powerhouse. His support for the project got him elected governor of New York by a landslide in 1817, yet there were many who didn't support the development of a canal they called "Clinton's Folly" or "Clinton's Big Ditch." Construction on the canal began on July 4, 1817 and lasted about 8 years. The effect of the canal was immediate and dramatic. Settlers poured into the Finger Lakes and western New York. Goods were transported at one-tenth the previous fee in less than half the time. Barges of farm produce and raw materials traveled east, as manufactured goods and supplies flowed west. In 1828, the Cayuga-Seneca Canal connected these two largest of the Finger Lakes with the Erie Canal.

*Factoid*:  Over time the use of the canal diminished as railroads boomed and became the dominant mode of transportation and shipping. While some parts of the Canal are still in use, most of the activity comes from tourists and other recreational users, and it has become a National Heritage Corridor administered by the National Park Service.

## "CONDENSED" HISTORY

In 1897, John T. Dorrance developed a commercially viable method for condensing soup, eliminating much of the water without reducing the flavor or nutritional value.  Within five years, his employer, the Campbell Soup Company, was selling more than 15 million cans of soup annually. On Thanksgiving Day, 1897, Campbell's comptroller, Herberton L. Williams, a spectator at the annual Cornell-Penn football game, was so impressed by the striking colors of Cornell's red and white uniforms, he suggested that his company replace the soup label's original black and orange design.  Williams' enthusiasm was formidable enough to convince management at Campbell's to adopt the Cornell colors, a design that endures on the classic line of soups to this day.

*Factoid*:  Pop artist Andy Warhol savored the icons produced in America, none more than the Campbell's soup can.  Among Warhol's most popular works, "Andy Warhol's Campbell's Soup Cans" is in the permanent collection at the Johnson Museum at Cornell University in Ithaca.

## GREAT AWAKENING

The Finger Lakes region was the site of the Second Great Awakening, a 19th century revival of Christianity; and the birth of new forms of spirituality and religion.  In the Seneca County town of Fayette on April 6, 1830, Joseph Smith organized the Church of Christ in a log home owned by Peter Whitmer, Sr.  Whitmer was one of five others besides Smith who were initial members of the Latter Day Saint movement started by Smith, later be known as The Church of Jesus Christ of Latter-Day Saints or the Mormon Church. The current house is a replica of the original log cabin and at its original site, open year-round for public tours.

*Factoid*: In the late 1820s, Brigham Young moved from Vermont to the Finger Lakes to work as a laborer on the Erie Canal. He was drawn to Mormonism after reading *The Book of Mormon* shortly after its publication in 1830. Young was ordained a member of the original Quorum of the Twelve Apostles in 1835, and after the assassination of Joseph Smith in 1844, he was chosen leader of the Mormons. Facing persecution in New York, he and his followers trudged across the country, arriving in the Salt Lake Valley on July 24, 1847.

## THE LOST HAMLET

As the wealthiest Ithacans of their time, the Treman family owned some the area's most treasured land, and in 1920, Robert H. Treman, donated a 387-acre parcel in Enfield Glen to the state for the development of a public park. First called Enfield Glen Reservation, in 1939 it was renamed in honor of its benefactor. As the state made improvements and added parking, many of the last remaining buildings of the upper park were razed. Two buildings survive from this "agricultural service hamlet," the Old Mill and the Miller's Cottage, both built about 1839. The mill is now a museum, revealing how flour was produced in this mill and the role the mill played in the surrounding agricultural community. The exhibit room on the first floor pays tribute to the men of the CCC camp who improved the park during the Great Depression.

*Factoid*: Since 1998, students from the Cornell University Interdisciplinary Archaeology Program have been engaged in a series of archaeological digs at the park, unearthing the history and the buildings of the hamlet of Enfield Falls. There is an archaeology walking trail marking the sites of all the buildings that have been excavated. Visitors step inside the granite footprints to get a feel for the size of these 19th century homes.

## NOW WE'RE TALKING

Theodore Case was born in Auburn on December 12, 1888, attended St. John's Northwestern Military Academy and St. Paul's School before studying physics at Yale and Harvard University. He began experiments with photographing sound waves while a student at Yale, and in 1916 he set up the Case Research Laboratory in a greenhouse at his Auburn estate. During World War I he worked on classified projects involving infrared signals for the US Navy. Case was instrumental in developing the first workable sound-on-film system, and in 1926 he joined forces with Hollywood studio mogul William Fox to form the Fox-Case Corporation for the production of talkies.

*Factoid*: In 1936 Case donated his Auburn home at 203 Genesee Street to the county to serve as the Cayuga Museum of History & Art. His laboratory has been preserved as he left it.

## FIRST OF MANY FIRSTS

Born in Auburn on January 9, 1916, Jerome Heartwell "Brud" Holland was dubbed "Brudder" by one of his twelve siblings, and the shortened version became his lifelong nickname. A 6-foot, 215-pound end with sprinter speed, Brud was the first African-American to play on the Big Red football field at Cornell University, and was chosen a first-team All American in 1937 and 1938. He was also the first African American to chair the American Red Cross Board of Governors, which named its Laboratory for the Biomedical Sciences in his honor. He was the first African-American to sit on the board of the New York Stock Exchange, and the first appointed to Massachusetts Institute of Technology's governing body.

Factoid: In 1970 President Richard Nixon named Holland the U.S. Ambassador to Sweden. This was a rare "second" for Holland; he was the second African American assigned as ambassador to a European nation.

## HANGING VALLEYS

Ithaca's "hanging valleys" are routes of streams that plunge into the lake below, eroding deep gorges into hillside siltstone and shale, transported downstream in tributary streams. These tributary streams were left "hanging" after the Ice Age. Hard rocks resist erosion, while soft rocks are worn away. When a hard lip overhanging softer rocks breaks off and crashes downward, a waterfall is created. No matter where you are in Ithaca, you are never far from the sight and sound of falling water – there are more waterfalls within 10 miles of downtown than any other city in North America.

*Factoid*: Among the most notable are Buttermilk Falls, taking its name from the frothy white cascade, and Devil's Kitchen Falls, the 28-foot wide crest of Lucifer Falls, plunging 115 feet over the gorge at Upper Treman Park.

## A DOG'S SECOND BEST FRIEND

Birsill Holly Jr. was born on November 8, 1820 in Auburn, after his father had moved the family there to become part of the crew constructing the new prison. Holly followed a job offer to Seneca Falls in his early twenties and became one of the partners of a new firm manufacturing hydraulic machinery and steam-powered fire engines. In 1849 he received his first patent for a rotary water pump, and is credited with co-invention of the Silsby steam fire engine in 1855. Ultimately over a thousand were produced, making it the most popular steam fire engine built in the United States. Holly patented 150 inventions in his lifetime, but he is best known for inventing the fire hydrant, patented in 1869.

*Factoid*: Holly became a friend of Thomas Edison. The renowned inventor once asked Holly to become an assistant at his research laboratory in Menlo Park, but he refused, wishing to concentrate on his own inventions.

## THE EYES HAVE IT

The ophthalmoscope is a device used as part of an eye examination, crucial in determining the health and proper function of the retina. Charles Babbage invented the ophthalmoscope in 1847, and Hermann von Helmholtz reinvented it in 1851, but the first hand-held direct illuminating ophthalmoscope, precursor of the device now used by clinicians around the world, was perfected in 1915 by Francis A. Welch and William Noah Allyn who founded a company in Skaneateles to produce them. Ophthalmoscopy has become one of the most ubiquitous medical screening techniques in the world today.

*Factoid*: Fourth generation family-owned Welch Allyn Inc., still headquartered in Skaneateles, is recognized worldwide as a leader and innovator in medical and dental diagnostics and remote visual inspection.

## RESTAURANT IN THE MIDDLE OF NOWHERE

If you're traveling the back roads of the Finger Lakes, and happen upon 4592 Grange Hall Road outside of Moravia, you will discover the region's most unusual restaurant. Niles Gourmet Bistro, a rustic, eccentric cucina, is the personal project of Sandie and Eric Becker. The blackboard menu includes an unexpected array dishes from the wood-fired stove in Sandie's kitchen or the brick oven out back. There are only four tables, so call ahead, (315) 784-5015, and let Sandie know you're coming. And prepare for a one-of-a-kind dining experience.

*Factoid*: This out-in-the-middle-of-nowhere log cabin includes one of the most interesting specialty markets in the area with local products available for purchase.

## WILD ABOUT HARRY

On one weekend each October, Ithaca's downtown becomes all things Harry Potter. Streets close and merchants spring up on every corner, as aspiring witches and wizards take part in pop-up activities like Wizard Chess, Sorting Hat, Wand Dueling, Dark Arts Coffee Tour, and Horcrux scavenger hunt. A costume contest for children and adults includes best mashup (think *Harry Potter* meets *Lord of the Rings*), best duo or group cosplay, and best original creation. Attendees can also participate in crafts with a Slime Potion and Dragon Egg booth.

*Factoid*: In 2018, Warner Brothers Studio, owner of the *Harry Potter* franchise, sent a letter to Wizarding Weekend in Ithaca, prohibiting the selling or representing anything under the Harry Potter name.

## A LEAP TO THE JEEP

John North Willys was born on October 25, 1873 in Canandaigua. As a young man he began selling bicycles in his hometown and within a few years eventually expanded into manufacturing his own line of bicycles. In 1897 he established a car dealership in Elmira, selling the Overland brand of automobiles. Willys bought the Overland Automotive Division of Standard Wheel Company in 1908 and in 1912 named it the Willys-Overland. He proved an astute operator and quickly turned the company's sagging fortunes around. By the time he acquired a 7-story headquarters in Toledo in 1915, Willys was the second largest carmaker in America. In 1930 John Willys, a strong supporter of the Republican Party, was appointed U.S. Ambassador to Poland by President Hoover.

*Factoid*: John Willys died in 1935 and never saw the birth of the Willys MB, designed by Willys-Overland's chief engineer Delmar "Barney" Roos. Commonly known as the Jeep, it was the world's first mass-produced four-wheel drive car, the primary light wheeled transport vehicle of the United States Military and its Allies in World War II, as well as the postwar period.

## AMERICA'S MOST UNIQUE POSTAL ROUTE

Under contract with the United States Postal Service, during July and August each year, a mailboat delivers letters and packages to twenty lakeside cottages around Skaneateles Lake that cannot be accessed by roads. The tradition began in the late 1800s and has continued uninterrupted, except during the two World Wars. The largest mail recipient is Camp Lourdes, at Ten Mile Point, the Roman Catholic Diocese of Syracuse summer retreat.

*Factoid*: Since 1982, mail deliveries have been made by the Barbara S. Wiles, a boat named for Barbara Stickley Wiles of the Stickley furniture family.

## SOCK IT TO ME

Built in 1844, the imposing limestone structure on Fall Street in Seneca Falls was originally the home of the Seneca Knitting Mill Company. By 1861, the Knitting Mill had a workforce of between three and four thousand men and women, turning out four thousand pairs of socks every day. The mill supplied woolen goods to the United States Army during the Civil War, throughout the two World Wars, then went on make specialty socks for players in the National Hockey League, the National Basketball League, and for NASA astronauts during spaceflight. Seneca Knitting Mill socks were the first footwear on the moon. After 155 years of continuous operation, the mill closed in 1999.

*Factoid*: While the initial employees of the Knitting Mill were almost strictly male, the tide changed and eventually the mill employed mostly women who operated the knitting machines. Fittingly, the mill building has become home of the National Woman's Hall of Fame.

## SIGN OF THE DOVE

Arthur Garfield Dove attended Hobart College and Cornell University, where he was chosen to illustrate the university yearbook. After graduating from Cornell in 1903 he became a successful commercial illustrator in New York City, working for *Harper's Magazine* and *The Saturday Evening Post*. In his use of a wide range of media, sometimes in unconventional combinations to produce his abstractions and his abstract landscapes, Dove is often considered the first American abstract painter.

*Factoid*: Built in 1878, by Dove's father, William, a successful brick manufacturer, the three-story commercial structure at the intersection of Castle and Exchange Streets in Geneva, once served as the artist's studio.

## TRACES OF THE PAST

Drumlins are small, low, rounded hills that make the landscape look like a gently rolling blanket. These low hills are made of till – deposits of boulders and pebbles – formed at the end of the last Ice Age when the great ice sheets that covered the Finger Lakes melted. The hills are steeper on the upstream end, the direction from which the ice flowed. In height, they rarely exceed 200 feet. There are thousands of drumlins across the northern Finger Lakes. One well-known example is Hill Cumorah, near Palmyra, where Joseph Smith reported a vision that led him to found the Mormon Church.

*Factoid*: Kettle lakes were formed when blocks of ice, buried in the outwash in front of the glacier, melted. As the glacier retreated northward, the stagnant ice broke off and was buried in the accumulating sediment. Dryden Lake on Route 38, south of Cayuga Lake, is a kettle lake.

## PET RENTAL

The world's first cat café opened its doors in Taipei, Taiwan, in 1998. The Taiwanese café eventually became a tourist destination, spawning cat cafés all over the globe. Sip coffee or tea with pastries and sandwiches at the Alley Cat Café at 312 East Seneca Street in Ithaca, then pay a cover fee of $5 for thirty minutes in the cat room. Cats and kittens are rescued by Browncoat Cat Rescue and are available for adoption.

*Factoid*: Cat cafés can be seen as a form of supervised indoor pet rental. Since cats have been proven to reduce depression and anxiety, the cat café concept ensures that people who aren't meeting their needs can come and have a "positive emotional experience."

## HAVE STAGECOACH, WILL TRAVEL

Born in Massachusetts in 1769 and a veteran of the Revolutionary War, Isaac Sherwood came to New York to work as a mail carrier. He soon used his familiarity with local routes to branch out into the stagecoach business. His stage lines from Albany to Buffalo, carrying passengers, letters, light packages and money, contributed to the rapid growth of industry and commerce in the Finger Lakes region. By 1807, he had also ventured into the hotel trade, building a tavern and stage coach house in Skaneateles. He is best remembered today as the namesake of the historic Sherwood Inn, which overlooks the northern end of Lake Skaneateles.

*Factoid*: The Spanish Flu of 1918 was the most devastating epidemic in recorded world history. The Finger Lakes was not immune to its ravages, and with area hospital capacity overwhelmed, the Sherwood was converted into a makeshift infirmary.

# HUNT-AND-PECK

In September of 1873, the Remington No. 1 became the first ever commercially produced typewriter, also the first to have the QWERTY keyboard that is still used today rather than an alphabetically arranged keyboard. Mark Twain is said to have been the first American novelist to produce a manuscript on the typewriter. In 1909, the company with roots in the original Remington Arms Company became Remington-Rand, the country's largest producer of typewriters. The factory on the south edge of Elmira employed more than 6,000 workers during World War II when the company converted its manufacturing processes to build the Norden Bombsite, a system that allowed it to directly measure the aircraft's ground speed and direction. The device was used in bombing missions over Germany and Eastern Europe by the Allies.

*Factoid*: Remington-Rand had a huge backlog of civilian orders to fill when the war came to an end. In 1945, the Elmira plant produced 2,500 typewriters and 700 adding machines a week to try to catch up on the orders. In 1972, however, the Remington-Rand plant closed for good, unable to compete with cheaper machines being manufactured overseas.

## ROLL OUT THE BARREL

Born in Auburn on October 24, 1838, Annie Edson met her husband, David Taylor, after taking a job as a teacher, but after 7 years of marriage, he was killed while fighting in the Civil War, leaving her a widow. She felt rootless and moved from teaching job to teaching job never really settling down. Turning sixty years old and more desperate to make ends meet, she decided she would be the first person to ride over Niagara Falls in a barrel. She had a custom oak barrel sized specifically for her, including straps with a combination of pillows and mattresses to break her fall, and on October 24, 1901 she was set adrift near the American shore, south of Goat Island.

The Niagara River currents carried the barrel over the Canadian Horseshoe Falls. Rescuers reached her barrel shortly after the plunge, and she was discovered to be alive. At age 63, Annie Edson Taylor became the first person to survive a trip over Niagara Falls in a barrel.

*Factoid*: Annie briefly earned money speaking about her experience, but was never able to cash in on the stunt. Her manager, Frank M. Russell, ran away with her barrel, and most of her savings were used towards private detectives hired to find it. The barrel was eventually located in Chicago, only to permanently disappear some time later.

## A KISS BEFORE YOU GO

The Cornell University suspension bridge that stretches 138 feet across Ithaca's Fall Creek, connecting students who live on North Campus to Central Campus, was designed by S.C. Hollister, Dean of Engineering, and Professor William McGuire, an expert on structural collapses. The construction contract was awarded to Bethlehem Steel Company, builders of the Golden Gate and George Washington Bridges. It was opened for use on January 7, 1961.

*Factoid*: Campus legend claims that refusing a midnight kiss while crossing the suspension bridge will cause the span to crumble and drop into the gorge.

## BAH HUMBUG!

Ebenezer Scrooge roams the streets, scowling at unsuspecting passers-by, and a cast of characters from Charles Dickens' *A Christmas Carol* interact with residents and visitors in a Victorian street party, complete with actors as Bob Cratchit, the Ghosts of Christmas Past and Present and the Ghost of Jacob Marley. Horse drawn carriages clip-clop through shouted snippets of Dickens' prose. Queen Victoria and St. Nicholas arrive.

"Dickens Christmas" has been an annual tradition in the village of Skaneateles since 1993, conducted weekend afternoons between Thanksgiving and Christmas, attracting more than 20,000 tourists each year.

*Factoid*: Produced by Scarlett Rat Entertainment, Dickens Christmas has a cast of about 70, who adopt thick British accents and burst into spontaneous Christmas carols, drink cider and wassail and nibble roasted chestnuts offered by shops and restaurants. The show comes together in just six rehearsals.

## RAGS TO RICHES

Thomas Jacob Hilfiger is the second eldest of nine children from a working-class Irish Catholic neighborhood in Elmira. While still in high school, Tommy would trek down to New York City and bring back odd-lot jeans to sell out of a storefront basement. In 1975, he opened a store on Aurora Street in downtown Ithaca called "People's Place," and although he had no formal training, he designed vests and sweaters to supplement jeans and bell-bottoms. The store was poorly managed, and in 1977, Tommy was forced to declare bankruptcy. He picked up the pieces and headed to New York City with wife Susan (who he met when she applied for a job at the Ithaca store). As luck would have it, Mohan Murjani, license holder of Gloria Vanderbilt jeans, offered to back Tommy's start-up company, and within a year Tommy Hilfiger, Inc. went public, extending into 40 product lines, including fragrances, belts, bedding, home furnishings, and cosmetics.

*Factoid*: Twenty years later the Hilfiger company had 5,400 employees and revenues in excess of 1.8 billion dollars. In 2006, Tommy sold his company for 1.6 billion dollars to a private investment company, Apax Partners.

## SUNFLOWER FIELDS FOREVER

At Frederick Farms at 2090 McBurney Road in Clifton Springs, just north of Seneca Lake, 700,000 sunflowers bloom across the rolling hills. When they reach peak color in mid-August, the perennial plants explode into a sea of shimmering yellow, one of the most impressive visual wonders of the Finger Lakes. John and Jan Frederick offer wagon rides through the sunflower fields on the second and third weekends in August.

*Factoid*: During growth, sunflowers tilt during the day to face the sun, but stop once they begin blooming. This tracking of the sun in young sunflower heads is called heliotropism.

## ANGEL INVESTOR SPREADS WINGS

Edwin Barber Morgan was born in Aurora on May 2, 1806 and attended the local Cayuga Lake Academy. At an early age he showed considerable business acumen, working in his father's store in the village, before establishing his own business in buying and shipping agricultural products. He built the Aurora Inn in 1833 and was an early investor in Henry Wells' American Express Company as well as Wells, Fargo & Company. Morgan also funded many local enterprises, including the construction of steamboats and the Oswego Starch Company, as well as the Cayuga Lake Railroad Company, whose route passed along the Aurora lakeshore.

*Factoid*: Another of Morgan's investments was a fledgling New York City newspaper. Within a few years, he held controlling shares of *The New York Times*. He supported the paper in its efforts to expose the corruption of the notorious Tweed Ring, which led to the arrest and imprisonment of "Boss Tweed."

# THE SECRET TO HOPPINESS

Hops are used in brewing to add bitterness, flavor, and aroma to beer. In the 19th century, New York State was the largest hops producer in the U.S. and farms across the Finger Lakes were the epicenter of hop production. Then came Prohibition. And about the same time, New York's hops were struck by a devastating mildew. By the end of the 1920s, the industry was nearly wiped out. In 2012, the New York State legislature in passed the Farm Brewery Bill, providing incentives to craft breweries that source at least 20 percent of each beer's ingredients from within the state. As a result, the Finger Lakes has enjoyed a boom in hop farming.

*Factoid*: Throughout the region, rows of 20-foot-tall trellises or thick poles holding up wires, like an outsized grape trellis. Growers run strings between ground and wire so that the hops plants can grow up the string.

# WOMEN ON PEDESTALS

According to the Smithsonian, out of the estimated 5,193 public statues on display throughout the United States, only 394 of these monuments are of women. In 1939, artist and sculptor Jean MacKay Henrich produced a female statue for the Veterans Memorial in Geneva's Pulteney Park, sculpted out of Georgian pink marble. Her official name is "Peace," and she is positioned in the center of a stone fountain dedicated in memory of the veterans of the Civil War, the Spanish- American War and World War I.

*Factoid*: Among other statues of women in the Finger Lakes, the National Women's Hall of Fame in Seneca Falls is home to sculptor Lloyd Lillie's life-size bronze figures of the five women who organized the First Women's Rights Convention.

# THE STONE GARDENER

Beginning in the mid-1980s, Wayne Myers began a 30-year transformation of his family property in Spencer, just south of Ithaca, into six acres of rolling lawn and horticultural display gardens with more than 550 different varieties of plants in a sculpture park of fieldstone walls and outbuildings. Myers' Gardens includes a covered bridge, a working water wheel on a post-and-beam-constructed feed mill, and a blacksmith shop. One of the jaw-dropping results of Myers' construction efforts is the massive amount of loose laid stonework of walls, stone bridges, and a 30-foot sundial with a 7-foot gnomon on a terrace built from 56 tons of stone.

*Factoid*: An unofficial tourist attraction, Myers' Garden is located at 1017 Michigan Hollow Road (corner of Hillview Road) on the border of Spencer and Danby. There are no set hours, but Myers gives tours if he's at home.

# BACK TO THE PAST

Since the early 1970s, Yates County has attracted Amish and Mennonite families in search of affordable farmland. A majority of the Mennonite population is now engaged in agriculture and operates an astounding 99 percent of the region's dairy farms. The Amish live very simply, farming modest plots of land, traveling by horse and buggy, wearing hand-sewn clothes, and avoiding anything driven by a gasoline engine or electricity. Farms with large families and many children eliminate the need for hired hands. While these Old Order lifestyles seem a bit odd, they are seeking to preserve a way of life that took root centuries ago.

*Factoid*: New York is experiencing a dramatic growth in horse-and-buggy driving populations, clip-cloping along the region's highways, with the largest gain of households of any state between 2006 and 2010.

# SHAKE HANDS WITH THE DEVIL

The Black Hand was a criminal extortion racket established by Italian immigrants in the United States during the 1880s, largely victimizing fellow immigrants by the use of scare tactics. Operations were firmly established in the Italian-American communities of major cities including New York, and by in the early 1900s the Black Hand had reached into Italian neighborhoods in the Finger Lakes. The May 27, 1908 issue of *The Geneva Daily Times* reported that the 16 Elm Street home of a local fruit wholesaler, Phillip Lanasa, was dynamited. He failed to heed the money demands made in a letter, sent with a dagger and body parts crudely drawn on it and signed with the mark of the Black Hand.

*Factoid*: Typical Black Hand tactics involved sending a letter to a victim threatening bodily harm, kidnapping, arson, or murder. The letter demanded a specified amount of money to be delivered to a specific place. Although more successful immigrants were usually targeted, as many as 90% of Italian immigrants and workmen were threatened with extortion.

# PUFF'S DADDY

One night in 1959, inspired by an Ogden Nash story titled, *The Tale of Custard the Dragon*, a Cornell University student named Leonard Lipton dashed off a poem he called "Puff, the Magic Dragon." A fellow student, Peter Yarrow, president of the Cornell Folk Music Club, later put music with the words, and Yarrow began performing the song as part of the folk group Peter, Paul and Mary.

*Factoid*: "Puff, the Magic Dragon" was recorded in 1963 by the group and is so well-known that it has entered American pop culture.

# HUNTING FOR DINNER

You'll have to hunt for Elderberry Farm. For three decades, Lou and Merby Lego have grown a variety of vegetables, fruits, herbs, and flowers at one of the most diverse certified-organic farmsteads at 3712 Center Street Road in Sennett, a small village located roughly halfway between Auburn and Skaneateles. In 2004, the Legos made the leap from farmers to restaurateurs, installing their Culinary Institute-trained son Chis in the kitchen. The Restaurant at Elderberry Farm is a culinary experience unlike any other in the Finger Lakes. While many regional restaurants make an effort to connect with local farms, the Elderberry Pond enterprise is a study in micro-locavorism, completely erasing the line from grower to chef.

*Factoid*: The restaurant menu features freshly harvested fruits, vegetables, herbs, and pasture-raised meats from the farm. Earthy fingerling potatoes are freshly-dug each morning, and salad greens are picked, leaf by leaf, just before opening time. Even the table flowers are picked daily from cutting gardens across the road from the restaurant.

# BURGUNDIAN OBSESSION

Only rarely do American wines hint at the real Burgundian poetry of Pinot Noir grown on limestone. Winemaker Tom Higgins spent countless hours poring over old geological maps, soil maps, quarry maps, and traversing up and down the Finger Lakes in the quest for limestone-rich soil, the holy grail to Pinot Noir vintners. Then, ten miles south of the north end of Cayuga Lake, he discovered a band of sedimentary rock called the Onondaga limestone escarpment. The presence of limestone deposits, heavy with nutrients from marine and shell fossils dating back millions of years ago, provided a perfect vineyard site for the Heart & Hands Wine Company. The result of Higgins' search are not-to-be-missed bottles of estate-grown "Mo Chuisle" Pinot Noir. The designation is a transliteration of an Irish expression for "my pulse."

*Factoid*: According to wine critic Robert Parker, ascribing all positive wine traits to terroir is called the "Burgundian obsession."

## ONCE UPON A TIME

Everyone knows the story about the great big father bear, a middle-sized mother bear and tiny baby bear. Three Greek Revival-style buildings that make up the courthouse complex in the Seneca County village of Ovid remind local folks of the popular fairy tale. Built in 1845, "Papa Bear" is a two-and-a-half-story, three-by-four-bay, Neoclassical structure with a portico supported by four Doric columns and topped with a cupola. "Mama Bear," also constructed in 1845, is similar in design and construction. "Baby Bear" was constructed about 1860 in the same, simple Doric design. The three graduated brick buildings dominate a sloping hillside park in the village.

*Factoid*: Ovid sits midway on a five-mile stretch of land between the two; the narrowest gap separating the lakes as they curve toward each other, and the cupola on top of Papa Bear offers a view of both Cayuga and Seneca Lakes.

## VEGETABLES FOR SPORT

The International Rutabaga Curling Championship takes place annually at the Ithaca Farmers Market. On the third Saturday in December, contestants are encouraged by cheering crowds as they pitch numbered rutabagas toward a parking cone 80 feet away. Once a rutabaga has been thrown, it remains on the field of play until other contestants have rolled, subject to being knocked by subsequent rolls. The contestant whose vegetable survives closest to the target is declared the winner.

*Factoid*: The rutabaga is sometimes called the Rodney Dangerfield of vegetables (since it "gets no respect"). Although there were early attempts to include other projectiles in the contest, rules were formalized to restrict anything but that much-maligned cross between cabbage and turnip.

## HELL ON EARTH

Elmira was the home of the North's most notorious and infamous Civil War prison. A quiet downtown neighborhood now occupies the site once occupied by rows of wooden bunk houses that held prisoners from July 1864 through July 1865. Nicknamed "Hellmira" by its inmates, the camp was a virtual death hole. It was built to hold 6,000 prisoners but took in 12,000. Conditions were toxic. In the first year of the camp, 3,000 of the 12,000 inmates died of insufficient food, bouts of dysentery, typhoid, pneumonia, smallpox, inadequate medical care and flooding of the Chemung River. A New York State historical marker on a one-way section of Water Street memorializes this sad and tragic chapter in Elmira's past.

*Factoid*: An observation platform with chairs and binoculars was built outside the prison camp across Water Street west of Hoffman Street. Visitors were charged 10 cents to look at the prisoners. Refreshments were sold to spectators while the Confederate soldiers starved.

## THE WATERFALL EFFECT

Philosopher Rudolf Steiner explained that forces of the living earth "influence the human being in various ways." In the hundreds of waterfalls around the Finger Lakes, from small cascades to hundred-foot high drops, when water falls on rock, it splits normally neutral particles into negatively -charged air molecules or ions. Once breathed into our systems, they produce a biochemical reaction that increases levels of the stress-relieving, mood-enhancing chemical serotonin.

*Factoid*: Serotonin plays a part in the creation of new brain cells, called neurogenesis, a vital function on the path to enlightenment. There are over 150 waterfalls within 10 miles of downtown Ithaca, sparking *The Utne Reader* to name Ithaca "America's most enlightened town."

## LAMPOON TYCOON

Edward Sanford Martin was born on January 2, 1856 at "Willowbrook," the Owasco Lake estate of his grand-uncle Enos Thompson Throop, the tenth Governor of New York (the Cayuga County town of Throop is named in his honor). As a child in a large and socially prominent family, the stream of notable visitors to his home included Ulysses S. Grant, William H. Seward, George Armstrong Custer, Washington Irving. Admiral David Farragut, and Jenny Lind, the "Swedish Nightingale," who sang by a grove at the lakefront. He completed secondary education in 1872 at Phillips Academy and in 1877 graduated with a bachelor's degree from Harvard University, where in 1876 he was one of the founders of the school's famed satirical review, *The Harvard Lampoon*. In 1883, he and fellow Harvard grads created *Life* magazine, originally intended as a humor magazine with limited circulation.

*Factoid*: Martin wrote so powerfully about World War I that he was named a Chevalier of the Legion of Honor by the French government.

## THE LOT OF FUN

Harry Eugene Roach was born in Elmira on January 14, 1892, the grandson of Irish immigrants. He had his name legally changed to "Hal" as a young adult, as he made his way to Hollywood, California, where he began working as an extra in silent films. After coming into a generous inheritance, he began producing short film comedies in 1915, and eventually purchased what became Hal Roach Studios, a fourteen-acre lot known as "The Lot of Fun." Roach created the enormously popular Our Gang comedy franchise and, fortuitously, teamed Stan Laurel and Oliver Hardy, who became one the most beloved comedy teams in cinema history. Other performers who worked at the studio included Will Rogers, Harry Langdon, Charley Chase, Patsy Kelly, Thelma Todd, Cary Grant, Jean Arthur, ZaSu Pitts and Jean Harlow.

*Factoid*: As a young boy, Roach met and shook hands with another master storyteller who lived in Elmira – Mark Twain.

## SAGA OF THE STEAMER

Seneca Falls was known for many years as the "Fire Engine Capital" of the Western hemisphere and perhaps the entire world. The Silsby Manufacturing Company, founded by H. C. Silsby in 1845, was called the "Island Works" because it was located on a five-acre island in the Seneca River in Seneca Falls. Silsby originally built agricultural implements, then moved to the application of steam to the suction and forcing of water in fire engines. As the factory expanded, its chief products became horse-drawn steam-pumper fire engines, hose carriages, hose carts, hose wagons, and Holly rotary pumps. The Silsby engine became the most popular steam fire engine in the country, saving countless lives and communities at a time when buildings were mostly made of lumber.

*Factoid*: During the steam era, Silsby manufactured more steam fire engines than any competitor, building well over 1000 machines. New York's last steam fire engine was withdrawn from service on May 26, 1933.

## FOREST FOR THE TREES

At one time, almost all of the northeastern U.S. was blanketed by the same, huge, hardwood forest. But by 1900, nearly all trees in the Finger Lakes had been cut down for farming, wood for buildings, roads, wagons, bridges, railroad ties, and paper. Intriguingly, there are patches of ancient forest ecosystems still tucked away in a very few places, undisturbed by farming or lumbering. One of those patches, a 35-acre parcel, can be found off Route 13, just south of Irhaca. With trees over 150-feet-tall, the Fischer Old-Growth Forest Natural Area (owned by Cornell University) is notable not only for the extreme size of many individual trees, but for the high number of tree species – at least 23 – of canopy size.

*Factoid*: The red blazed trail passes through young forest before entering an ancient forest with an exceptional diversity of tree species and sizes – many over 300 years old. This old-growth forest is considered the best of the few remaining pre-European settlement forests in the region.

## PORTRAIT OF THE ARTIST

Francis Bicknell Carpenter was born in the Cortland County village of Homer on August 6, 1830. After showing his father a painting of his mother, Carpenter was sent to Syracuse to study under Sanford Thayer. In 1852, Carpenter was commissioned to paint a portrait of President Millard Fillmore, followed by portraits of Presidents Franklin Pierce and John Tyler, and other mid-19th century notables, including the clergyman Henry Ward Beecher, newspaper editor Horace Greeley, Ezra Cornell, founder of Cornell University, James Russell Lowell, poet, and John C. Fremont, the first Republican presidential candidate.

*Factoid*: Carpenter is best known for his painting "First Reading of the Emancipation Proclamation of President Lincoln." He spent months in the White House, painting from life, as Lincoln worked. Another Homerite, William Osborn Stoddard, private secretary to Mr. and Mrs. Lincoln, assisted his friend Carpenter in getting the painting placed on view in the House wing of the Capitol in 1878. The painting now hangs in the west stairwell of the Senate wing.

# DISPENSE WITH THE PLEASANTRIES

A graduate of Wells College in Aurora, Pleasant Rowland went on to become the creator of the successful American Girl brand, manufacturer of dolls, books, clothing for dolls and girls, and numerous other accessories, including dollhouses and children's furniture. In 1998, after selling the company to Mattel for $700 million, she turned her attention to Aurora, donating her time and wealth to restoring properties and businesses throughout the village. She created an enterprise that included upscale accommodations at the Aurora Inn and the E. B. Morgan House, and restored more than 15 buildings. In 2001 Rowland purchased Aurora-based MacKenzie-Childs, the eccentric home decor company, reorganized and retrieved it from bankruptcy to profitability.

*Factoid*: Many locals were upset by Rowland's overhaul of the village. The tipping point came when she purchased the Fargo Bar, a treasured dive, and gentrified it.

# BACK FROM THE BRINK

With its snowy-feathered head and white tail, the eagle became the national symbol of the United States in 1782, yet the bird almost became extinct before the banning of the insecticide DDT. In the mid-1960s, the entire New York State bald eagle population consisted of just one single pair which nested at the south end of Hemlock Lake. To reestablish a breeding population, over a 13-year period the New York State Department of Environmental Conservation collected 198 bald eagle nestlings from areas with healthy populations, raised to independence with minimal human contact, and released in New York.

*Factoid*: The current breeding bald eagle population in New York State is estimated to be 323 breeding pairs.

# STUFFING THE CAT

Caesar Grimalkin, a gray tiger cat with seven toes on each white front paw, lived with Celia and William Hazlitt Smith and their 2-year-old daughter at 116 Oak Avenue in Ithaca. Celia's sister-in-law, Charity Smith, painted a likeness of the cat onto a three-piece pattern and created a stuffed cloth version based on his likeness. The design was patented in October 1892 and sold by the Smiths for one cent a yard to Arnold Print Works in Massachusetts, which then marketed the printed pattern as "The Tabby Cat" for Christmas in 1892. Nearly 200,000 were sold nationwide that first holiday season. The sew-at-home stuffed toy made appearances at the 1893 Chicago World's Fair and in the windows of Wanamaker's department store in Philadelphia. Advertisements and articles appeared in newspapers and magazines around the world. Ithaca Kitty preceded the Teddy Bear by a full 22 years.

*Factoid*: The stuffed toy was especially known for its lifelike appearance and was allegedly used by farmers to scare away birds and by the Central Park police station to frighten away mice.

# CHATEAUNEUF-DU-POPE

Located in Conesus near Hemlock Lake, O-Neh-Da Vineyard is the oldest dedicated sacramental winery in the United States, founded by the first Bishop of Rochester, Bernard J. McQuaid, in 1872. During Prohibition, O-Neh-Da was allowed to remain in the business of producing altar wine, unlike other wineries in the region. According to Canon Law, wine used for communion during religious Mass must be made with grapes and cannot contain extraneous substances, such as water, corn syrup, or cane sugars. Every three years, winery practices are reviewed and granted a letter of approbation, which testifies to the integrity and liturgical fitness of the wine. O-Neh-Da (the Seneca word for "Lake of Hemlock Trees") currently provides wine for Catholic, Orthodox, Episcopal and Lutheran churches around New York State.

*Factoid*: O-Neh-Da provided wine for the celebration of Mass by Pope Francis at Madison Square Garden in New York City on September 25, 2015.

## LATE BLOOMERS

Temperance activist and suffragette Elizabeth "Libby" Miller of Geneva began wearing loose trousers gathered at the ankles, inspired by the pantaloons of Turkey, and topped by a short dress or skirt and vest. Other   women in the area found the clothing sensible and less restricting, including her cousin Elizabeth Cady Stanton and friend Amelia Jenks Bloomer, who wrote about it in *The Lily*, a newspaper dedicated solely to women.  The trend was picked up by *The New York Tribune*, and throughout the 1850s, "bloomers" became a symbol of women's rights, a physical and metaphorical representation of feminist reform.

*Factoid*: The name survived for the knickerbockers women wore while riding bicycles in the cycling craze of the 1890s, and for women's loose, baggy underwear.

## THE VIKING OF 6TH AVENUE

Born in Marysville, Kansas in 1916, Louis Thomas Hardin was blinded at the age of 16 when a dynamite cap exploded in his face.  He studied music at the Iowa School for the Blind, where he learned to compose in braille.  In 1943, he moved to New York City and adopted the name "Moondog," inspired by his dog who howled at the moon.  As a street artist, he became a permanent fixture on 6th Avenue between 54th and 55th Street, wearing a cloak sewn from army blankets and Viking-style helmet, sometimes playing music or reciting poetry, but often just standing silent.

He rubbed elbows with Benny Goodman, Charlie Parker, Lester Young, and appeared on *The Tonight Show with Johnny Carson*. Moondog made his way to Candor, 15 miles south of Ithaca, where from 1958 to 1973 he divided his time between a hemlock shack at 230 Slate Road and New York City. After struggling to make a living as a musician in the states, in 1974 he moved to Germany where he spent the remainder of his life.

*Factoid*: Moondog's music was a strong influence on many early minimalist composers, and his work was championed by Artur Rodziński, conductor of New York Philharmonic. He collaborated with the young Philip Glass, was promoted by a top rock producer, and has been covered by artists as diverse as Janis Joplin and Antony and the Johnsons.

## THE BERNARD MADOFF OF HIS TIME

Born in the Livingston County town of Geneseo, Ferdinand DeWilton Ward Jr., son of the town's Protestant pastor, moved to New York City and in 1880 established the banking and brokerage firm Grant & Ward, making the business seem reputable by taking on a partner with name recognition. His partner was Ulysses S. Grant, Jr., son of President Grant, who knew little of what came to be called a "Ponzi scheme," promising investors improbable returns from unlikely investments, in Ward's case government procurement contracts. But there were no government contracts. The whole thing was a hoax. Ward used the same securities over and over again as collateral against loans. When the scheme collapsed in 1884, many investors were bankrupted, including editorial cartoonist Thomas Nast and President Grant who had invested his life savings with the firm. Ferdinand Ward became "the best-hated Man in the United States." He served six-and-a-half years of a ten-year sentence in Sing Sing Prison for fraud.

*Factoid*: Mark Twain spoke of cursing Ward "with all the profanity known to the one language I am acquainted with," as well as "odds and ends of profanity drawn from the other two languages of which I have a limited knowledge."

## BRICK SHITHOUSE

The Dr. John Quincy Howe House is a grand Victorian mansion on Main Street in the Ontario County town of Phelps. Built in 1869, the house features a two-story, six-hole (three up, three down) outhouse built of brick, thought to be the only structure of its kind anywhere in the United States. Access to the unique toilets can be gained from both first and second floors of the house.

*Factoid*: The Howe House was purchased in February 1999 and donated to the Phelps Community Historical Society and is now operated as a museum.

## NOTE

The job of a writer is to get things right, of course, but careful research and consultation with regional historians, there's always a chance I missed something. That's why I want to hear from you. Please send any comments, corrections, or suggestions you may have to:

michael.turback@gmail.com

and I will do my best to get it right in the next edition of this book.

www.ingramcontent.com/pod-product-compliance
Lightning Source LLC
Chambersburg PA
CBHW051252140626
46661CB00017B/121